HINDU SOCIETY—
AN INTERPRETATION

IRAWATI KARVE
Professor of Sociology and Anthropology,
Deccan College Postgraduate and Research Institute, Poona.

DECCAN COLLEGE, POONA

VIJAYADASHMI, 1961

Printed by M. H. PATWARDHAN at Sangam Press Private Ltd., 383
Narayan Peth, Poona 2 and published by S. M. KATRE, Deccan
College Postgraduate and Research Institute, Poona 6.

PREFACE

This book is the result of my deliberations on the data collected by me in the course of my field work in different parts of India during the last twenty years and of my perusal of the literature in Sanskrit, Prakrit and the modern Indian languages. Four articles entitled "What is Caste" published in the *Economic Weekly* of Bombay during 1958-59 presented some of my ideas in a very condensed form. They were further elaborated in a series of lectures which I gave before the South Asia Colloquium of the University of California at Berkeley in 1959-60. I am deeply indebted to many colleagues in India and the U.S.A., too numerous to be mentioned by name, for their criticism, suggestions and encouragement after reading the first draft. I must however mention the name of one who I was sure would have read this book and offered helpful comments as he did after he read my book on Kinship — I mean the late Professor Clyde Kluckhohn.

Poona,   I. K.

Vijayadashmi, 1961

INTRODUCTION

In this book Dr. IRAWATI KARVE sums up her lifetime work of investigating the structure and history of Indian society and in so doing she presents a series of important theories and conclusions which all persons interested in that subject need to consider with great attention. Her thoughts are based upon two main sources of information—extensive field research in many parts of India, but especially in her home land Maharashtra, and a study of pertinent material in Sanskrit and allied literature from the time of the Rig Veda. Associated with this has been copious reading in other scholars' work and weighing of others' social theories. Few investigators have had such excellent equipment for this kind of study and can present material which is so informative and suggestive.

Most of her attention is naturally given to the caste system. She opens with a chapter on the variety of behavioural patterns in Indian society, a phenomenon which is so extreme that it would be hard to explain by the traditional Hindu teaching that the proliferation of castes is the result of fission, sub-fission, sub-sub-fission, and so on, of a limited number of "original" castes—four or five—differentiated by occupation or function. That improbable view is rendered untenable on the basis of a number of considerations including her own study of blood types and other physical characteristics. From such studies and other considerations she finds it possible to define scientifically, rather than impressionistically, a typical caste (*jāti*) as an extended family, a kinship entity, hence endogamous, normally with a hereditary occupation. The inclusion of the caste system within the framework of the Vedic Aryan four-class (*varṇa*) society, which later became five-class, is an artificiality, as of course many other anthropologists hold, a Brahmanic rationalization unsupported by historical data or modern field research.

At this point Dr. KARVE argues for a pre-Aryan existence of the caste system or something like it. Others, especially students of the history of religion, have argued to this same end in the past, but Dr. KARVE bases her opinion on facts of caste distribution and differentiation, tribal practices, the ways in which non-Aryan tribes become castes in Aryan society, and the general non-Aryan, that is non-Vedic, character of medieval and modern Indian thought, religious dogma, and social institutions. She gives little weight to the Aryan Brahmanical emphasis upon religious ritual, and the incentive to preserve it, as an element in the formation of the system as a whole. Her theory is at present largely a hypothesis but it has the advantage of explaining some features of the caste system so far not otherwise explained, and as our knowledge extends, as of the Harappa culture, we may hope for more definite evidence pro or con than is now available.

The occupational aspect of caste, so much stressed in Sanskrit tradition, she associates with the Rigvedic notion of *vrata* as one's personal function and with the latter the notions of duty, that is, of one's *karma* (action) as one's *dharma* (duty), which is so well developed in the Bhagavad Gītā. With this she connects the magical *satyakriyā* (Truth Act) known in the Rigveda, Brahmanic, Buddhist, and Jain literature and even in more recent tales recorded in Tamil or other modern languages.

In speaking of the mechanisms by which caste has continued and flourished in India throughout three and possibly more millennia, Dr. KARVE comments on the rivalry between Brahman and Kshatriya for first place in the orders of society, and says that "the *varṇa* system, which appears so inflexible, itself is surprisingly flexible, because while the words denoting the five orders remained the same, the castes included in them changed." In short, the Brahmanic notion of inflexibility is unreliable. She also comments on cohesion among castes belonging to the same *varṇa* but again on factionalism among castes within a single *varṇa*.

Finally, Dr. KARVE presents her views on certain social problems which are current issues in modern India. These are associated with language, reform of the Hindu legal code dealing with women's position, the inviolability of the cow, communalism, prohibition, the emergence of new types of caste loyalty, preferential caste status in law, rights of Untouchables, movement of the population from villages to market towns and cities, the character of the newly established Panchayats, the ideals of democracy and freedom. As an anthropologist of great experience and thoughtfulness she deserves close attention when she speaks about such matters.

The remarks above may, I hope, give some idea of the range of Dr. KARVE's book and suggest its importance to students of both modern and ancient India as providing a constructive view of Indian society. It deserves wide reading.

University of Pennsylvania   W. NORMAN BROWN
Philadelphia,
June 12, 1961

Finally, Dr. Kern... devotes two pages to certain social problems which are encountered ... in modern India. These are associated with the growing... form of the Hindu ideal ... more dealing with women, a position, the inviolability of the low ... ... of caste ... prohibition, the emergence of new types of caste in the low ... ... status in low ... ... of... movement of the population from villages to ... ... and cities, the character of the new ... ... Panchayats, the ideals of democracy and freedom. As an anthropologist of great experience and insight ... ... close attention ... the people about such matters.

In the remarks above ... I have given some idea of the range of Dr. Kern's book ... ... its importance to students of both modern and ancient India, as providing a ... ... India ... ... It deserves wide circulation.

University of Pennsylvania
Philadelphia
... ... 1947

CONTENTS

1

THE VARIETY OF BEHAVIOURAL PATTERNS

The first impression that one gets of the Hindu society is the bewildering variety of behavioural patterns found in it. This impression persists and has been strengthened by a life-time of study of this society. Certain uniformities exist side by side with this variety. In my work on kinship organization I had tried to show that there are large regions in India where kinship organization was similar, but even as regards this cultural item there are small aberrations from the pattern within a region. In the United States, made up of ethnic elements from all over the world and where personal liberty is greatly valued, one finds greater variety in behaviour patterns than one does in European countries; but even in the United States bigamy has been prohibited by law, polyandry is not even heard of, all teaching is done through one language, and in spite of great liberty as regards dress no person will be allowed to go naked through the streets. This kind of uniformity has been absent in India with the result that almost every type of behaviour pattern recorded anywhere in the world has been found in India.[1] The variety embraces all aspects of life. How all-pervasive it is will be clear from the following few examples.

There is endless variety in the type of foods eaten and their preparation. Roughly each region eats what it grows, but in regions where more than one variety of cereals or pulses is grown, some eat exclusively some

---

[1] In recent years some of the variety has been reduced through state legislation. A reference to these measures will be made later.

varieties while others eat other varieties. How these
preferences and taboos work, can be illustrated from some
recent examples. In the year 1946-47 Bengal was hit by
a severe famine and food-grains were sent to the hungry
land from all over India. But the people of Bengal did
not know how to cook millets and wheat and so volunteers
had to be sent to teach them. However, the Bengalis did
not relish the new food and workers who had gone from
my city told me after their return how many Bengalis died
rather than accustom themselves to these new kinds of
food. In some regions of the Bombay State people, especially well-to-do people, eat wheat and rice. In the years
1940 to 1950, when food was rationed, each region was
supplied the type of food which it ate. In Poona, rice was
in short supply, so was wheat. But millets could be had
in adequate quantities. Neighbours of ours, who had
come from the Nagpur area, refused to eat what they
called "cattle-feed" and spent a lot of money in buying
wheat in the black market. In eastern Andhra both rice
and a kind of extremely small millet are grown. The farmer eats this latter grain and sells his rice, which is mostly
eaten by city people. I evoked surprise when I showed
preference for millet bread as against rice. I discovered
that it was a matter of prestige. In this area as soon as
a young man became a clerk in a city office, he started
eating rice, while much richer farmers stuck to their diet
of millet. The National Food Technological Laboratory in
Mysore has undertaken research for the manufacture of
rice-like material from the starch obtained in the form of
a paste from other cereals or tubers. Apart from prestige, variety arises from religious practices. In the Hindu
calendar there are a number of days on which fasting is
prescribed. These fast-days differ for different sects and
for the same sects in different regions. "Fast" may mean
a complete taboo on all foods or may mean the eating of
only certain special foods. The prescribed foods for a fast
change so much that what is special "fast" food for some
people is everyday food for others. This was brought
vividly to my notice when travelling in Andhra, where a

man who was "fasting", ate from our food things which
would have been taboo in our region. Even apart from
fasts, certain foods are tabooed by certain sects. Strict
Jains do not eat tubers or fresh vegetables. Among Maharashtra Brahmins elderly ladies and widows of all ages
were supposed not to eat onions and garlic.[2] Some religious sects prescribe a strictly vegetarian diet. Among
Jains meat, eggs and fish are tabooed. Among Hindus on
the other hand some castes are strictly vegetarian while
others eat meat. In Maharashtra non-Brahmins eat meat
and eggs and fish, while Brahmins are supposed to be vegetarians. But among Brahmins one caste, the Saraswats,
eat fish. The preparation of food, the way it is eaten and
the implements used differ from region to region and from
group to group. In the north and north-west of India
bread is made by grinding the grain in the dry condition
so as to give flour and then making a dough of the required
consistency by adding water. The dough is kneaded, rolled or patted and baked on a flat iron plate. In the south,
the south-west, and parts of the east, cereal (mainly rice
and pulses) is soaked in water and then made into a rough
paste by grinding on an oblong stone with another cylin-
drical stone or in a hollowed stone trough. Such a dough
does not allow itself to be rolled with a rolling pin and so
it is either cooked like dumplings or made into pancake-
like things. While the stone mill is a household implement
of the north, the flat stone grinder is that of the south.
These stone grinders are like the *matate* and *mano* of the
Mexican Indians. Wherever a south Indian goes he
carries these two with him. In the north vegetables are
cut by a knife. The thing to be cut is held in the left
hand, while the right hand holding the knife is moved up
and down in a chopping action. In the south, centre and
east, there is a big curved blade attached to a block of
wood, on which the cutter sits. The vegetables are held
in the two hands and then moved up and down on the

---

[2] I have to cook meals without onions when my mother is a guest
in our house.

cutter. The two implements have two different names, one
of Sanskritic origin and the other of Dravidian origin.
There is no common item of food in the daily food of all
Indians.

In the north, people of all castes will eat food from an
earthen vessel. In the south and centre, a Brahmin will
never use an earthen vessel either for cooking or for eating. In a recent survey of some Maharashtra villages
carried out by my colleagues and me, the possession and
use of earthenware gave an instrument for caste-rank-
ing. The same variety is found in dress — the types,
the colours, the number of garments worn, etc. The north-
west has tailored garments for men and women. In the
rest of India, the lower garment is just a varying length
of cloth and the upper garment may be tailored or may be
absent in many cases. In the whole of the north, central
and north-eastern regions, with the exception of bridal garments, women generally wear white clothes. Colourful-
ness increases as one goes southwards. In certain cul-
ture-contact regions this boundary is sometimes very
abrupt. In Orissa the north and the south meet somewhere on the coastal plain near Kalingapattanam. In all
Kalinga villages, women are dressed in white, in the nearby non-Kalinga villages women have coloured saries. The
kind of colours, the kind of borders, the mode of wearing
or printing enables a person to say where a particular garment comes from. Colours have different significance in
different parts of India. In the Punjab and Bengal a
bride is dressed in red. In the Maratha country, the colour
at the time of the ritual is yellow. Also in the Maratha
region green has a special significance not found elsewhere.
When a girl reaches puberty, the first sari presented to
her is green. During her wedding, except at the time of
the ritual, she wears green. When she is pregnant, she
wears green; when her son marries, she receives a green
sari as a gift from the bride's mother. Finally, if she dies
while her husband is living, she is cremated with a green
sari on. With the green sari go green bangles. A widow

must not have a thread of green in her garments. "It is a blessing to die in green" is a Marathi saying.[3]

Finally in the whole of the north and central India, men wear some kind of foot-wear. The words for foot-wear in all northern languages (*Vahan, Joda, Paytan, Jute*), are Sanskritic in origin. Apparently foot-wear was unknown in the south. There is no Dravidian word for foot-wear. The modern word, Sapaat, Chapata or Chapala, is supposed to have been derived from a Portuguese word, *zapote*.

The variety in family organization is equally great. Polyandry and polygyny are both found. There are groups which are matrilineal, others which are patrilineal. The taboo on consanguine marriages changes from region to region and from caste to caste. In the north marriage of cousins is not allowed; there are some regions in the centre and the south which allow one type of cross-cousin marriage and others allow both types of cross-cousin marriage. Finally there are regions which allow cross-cousin marriage and also the marriage of a man to his elder sister's daughter. The modes of inheritance and succession are also different.

The type of folk-tales and folk-songs changes from region to region, depending upon the kind of family organization it has. The sentiments expressed, the behaviour expected and the norms prescribed also change. A few days spent in a northern family and a southern family are enough to experience how different the whole atmosphere is in the two places.

The types of gods worshipped and the mode of worship change from region to region, and within one region from group to group and within one group from family to family. The two ends of Uttar Pradesh show allegiance to two different incarnations of the same deity. In eastern U.P. and in Bihar Rama is the beloved deity, while

---

[3] I am not talking of bygone practices. My mother-in-law was cremated in green; my widowed mother must always be given presents of saris which have no green in them.

in the west, near Mathura, Krishna is the popular deity.
The majority of names of people in the former region had
reference to Rama[4] (Rambharose, Ramkhilona, Ram-
prasad, Ramsinhasan, Ramhriday, etc.). South Bihar is
dedicated to Mahabir, the god Hanuman. People belonging to the same cult practise it in slightly different ways.
Among Vaishnavaites one finds the following varieties —
the worship of Krishna as Partha-Sarathi (the chariot-
driver of Arjuna) is found only in Tamilnad; temples of
Nṛsinha are found only in Maharashtra, Andhra and Karnatak. The names Narasinha, Narasayya for men are
also found only in these three regions. In Maharashtra
and Karnatak Vishnu is worshipped as Vithoo (Prakrit
form of Vishnu), though his wife is Rukmini, instead of
Laxmi. The worship of Kumara or Kartikeya, a son of
Shiva is found now only in the south. In Andhra and
Tamilnad this god is worshipped as Arumugam (six-
mouths) by men and women. In Maharashtra the sight
of this god is taboo to women.[5] There are some temples
of god Vishnu in his original form also. The worship of
the mother goddess in her innumerable forms differs from
region to region and from family to family. A further
study of this variety reveals certain important facts. In
India there is a literary record which goes back to about
1000 B.C. Vedic hymns, stories and ritual of the books
called Brahmaṇas, the thoughts of Upanishadas, Puranas,
story literature, dramas, poems in Sanskrit, and the stream
of literature which began some centuries later but ran side
by side with the main stream, namely the literature of the
Buddhists in the Pali and Sanskrit languages and the literature of the Jains in the Maharashtri and Ardhamagadhi
languages all show that beliefs and practices and behavioural patterns recorded in them are still extant in India. The

---

[4] I. KARVE — Personal Names in India, Bombay University School
of Economics & Sociology, *Jubilee Volume*, 1947.
[5] There is a temple of Kartikeya in Poona. The author has not
been able to go in. A sight of the god is supposed to make a
woman a widow for seven successive births.

early Vedic people mentioned some people by a term of contempt which meant "those who worship the male sexual organ" (Śiśnadeva). Possibly these were early worshippers of Shiva. Very soon Shiva, whose symbol is a phallus, became an honoured god in the pantheon. Later he became one of the Hindu trinity (Brahma, Vishnu and Shiva). Still later as the importance of Brahma vanished he became one of the two (Vishnu and Shiva) most worshipped deities of India. This position he still holds today. Benares, Shiva's city, has become the most sacred city of India. In this way other gods got added to the pantheon and whole books called Puranas were written in their praise. Skanda (called Subrahmanyam or Khandoba), Ganapati, Laxmi are some of these later gods and goddesses not found in the Vedas. The story literature mentions a host of spirits worshipped in villages and we find that they are still so worshipped. The important thing in this process is that while certain gods lose their importance and new ones rise, very few gods are lost entirely and finally. The sun-god still gets his oblation of flowers and a short prayer and has a sacred day (Sunday) on which some men and women fast in his honour. Indra the powerful Vedic god is no longer worshipped, but once a year in certain parts of India a pole is erected to do him honour. Varuna, the god of the waters, is appeased at the end of every rainy season by the citizens of Bombay who throw thousands of coconuts in the sea as offerings to him. Through three thousand years the Hindu pantheon has steadily grown. As new gods are added the old gods may wax or wane in importance but none are discarded for ever. The historical process is one of continuous accretion. There does not seem to be a stage where a choice was made between alternatives, a choice involving acceptance of one alternative and a definite, final rejection of the other.[6]

---

[6] There are instances of persons and sects who made such a choice but it never became general.

This is seen not only as regards worship of gods but as regards almost all aspects of social behaviour. The later literature every time adds a few more items as the writers became acquainted with different parts of India. At each stage a few new gods, a new type of marriage code, a new type of food or dress is mentioned as belonging to the society. New patterns were recorded and brought within the circle of permitted behaviour. It is a process of continuous addition, what I have called agglomeration. It is not as if nothing has vanished. One can find out a few things recorded in the past but not existing today, but their number is small. There does not seem to be any exercise of conscious choice, which always involves both rejection and acceptance. The new has not meant the rejection of the old. That is why I have called it a process of continuous accretion.

Part of this variety is due to regional differences. A country as big as India, with regions differing widely in climate and soils, in historical growth and in racial elements is bound to show differences in behaviour patterns but the variety cannot be explained as merely regional. Many patterns are found in one and the same region. To take but one example — in Kerala the Nambudri are a patrilineal, patrilocal people among whom it is customary for only the eldest and sometimes one other son to marry. The descent and inheritance are through males. The Nayars and some other people in the same region are matrilineal and matrilocal. There is a small group of goldsmiths called Asari who are patrilineal and polyandrous. There are Illava who are patrilineal and patrilocal and all sons and daughters marry and the sons inherit equally from the father. Thiyya are both patrilineal and matrilineal. All these people are Hindus, i.e., belong to one religion and make pilgrimages to the same sacred temples in the region. This variety is found even among primitive people as is described by Professor MANDELBAUM for the Nilgiri region where the Todas, Kotas and Badagas live. Each one of these groups has a different behavioural pattern.

Secondly, though there are large regions in which one cultural trait or a few complex common cultural traits can be found, they are never found without exception among all groups. Within a given cultural region there are always a few groups which differ in a few cultural items.[7]

As we shall see later there are certain aspects of life in which great freedom is allowed to the individual but the variety of behaviour described above is not due to personal liberty. Barring some items a person does not have choice as regards the model of behaviour he wants to follow. A person moves within rather narrow boundaries of behaviour traditional to the group of which he is a member. The source of behavioural variety is this group. There are hundreds of such groups and the mode in which they live together and have done so for centuries past will help to explain what I have termed above "a process of continuous accretion" as also the second feature of this society, namely, "the coexistence of a multiplicity of behaviour patterns."

These groups are known in modern anthropological literature as castes. *Jāti* is the word oftenest used in India but it is not understood all over the country. The author found that in parts of Andhra, Karnatak and Tamilnad the word *kulam* was used in some places side by side with *jāti*, in other places exclusively.[8] A caste is a group which practises endogamy, has a particular area (generally within one linguistic region) of spread or dispersion, may have one or more traditional occupations, has a more or less determinate or flexible position in a hierarchical scale and has traditionally defined modes of behaviour towards other castes. Recently the author has defined caste as an extended kin group. This has reference to the first of the features enumerated above. Because of constant endo-

---

[7] Linguistic regions by their very definition share one language but even in this respect, in the Indian society which is largely illiterate, pockets of languages different from the languages of the region do exist.

[8] In Sanskrit literature the words *jāti* and *kula* have different meanings but in many places in literature the word *kula* was used almost as a synonym for the word *jāti*.

gamy it is possible to demonstrate, at least for smaller
castes, that each family is connected by ties of blood and/
or marriage with the other families in the caste. An
endogamous social group being defined as "extended kin
group" might sound tautologous and obvious but the significance of this description will become apparent in two
respects. Occupation, rank and traditional area of the
spread of a caste have changed; but the one thing about
caste which seems more resistant to change is its kinship
character. It also helps to understand the similarity of
caste to a tribal group. I had also proposed that the word
caste should be used exclusively for this endogamous
group. There are generally in a linguistic area a number
of such endogamous groups or castes, each following the
same or similar occupation. I had proposed the word
caste-cluster for each such caste-group. To take one
example — in the Marathi-speaking area, there are Tirole
Kunbi, Dhanoje Kunbi, Konkani Kunbi and others who are
engaged in agriculture. Each one of these groups is a
caste and all taken together make a caste-cluster, called the
Kunbi-cluster. In the same way Chitpavan, Karhade,
Madhyandina, Kanva are some of the Brahmin castes. All
together would belong to the caste-cluster "Brahmins".
In the same way we can talk about the caste-cluster of the
Sonar (Goldsmith), Teli (Oil presser), Shimpi (Tailor),
etc. In certain contexts, especially with reference to rank
or similarity of functions, it becomes necessary to speak
about different clusters as belonging to some more inclu-
sive group. For example castes following occupations like
carpenters, brass-pot-makers, ironsmiths, goldsmiths, in
certain areas of India are in the habit of designating themselves as belonging to a comprehensive group of "artisans" ("The five", Panchal). In the same way certain
clusters of castes are called in modern literature "untouchables" or "scheduled castes". These groups of castes are
generally bigger and more varied than what we have called
"a caste-cluster". Such groups include several caste-
clusters and have reference to a certain rank or claimed
privileges. No special term need be given for this type of

grouping together of caste-clusters, but wherever reference is made to such groups the number of caste-clusters included in it will be indicated.

It has been noted above that castes are arranged in a hierarchical order. This order is of two types. One is an order in a small area (a village or a group of villages), where a given number of castes are arranged in an order which is recognized by the majority. Secondly, there has been in existence for at least 2500 years an order which rests historically on a classification of society by ancient Hindu theoreticians. This order divides all Hindus into four primary classes called *varna*. It would be best to use this word for the theoretical order. Indian literature recognises only two groupings. Single endogamous castes called *jāti* and the four ancient orders in which they are grouped, namely *varna*. There are no words for caste-clusters denoting a group of castes following the same occupation or higher complexes made up of several caste-clusters. If a caste were only an endogamous group in a fourfold order, words for grouping of castes would not have been necessary. But a caste, besides being an endogamous unit, is also a status group and an occupational and economic group and it is necessary to understand groupings of castes besides those under the *varna* system for an understanding of the working of the caste society. We shall consider this point later on.

Of the three types of groups — castes, caste-clusters and *varna* — referred to above, it is the caste which is mainly responsible for the variety in behavioural patterns found in India. In English anthropological literature the word caste was used for what I have termed the caste-cluster or even sometimes for *varna*. The smaller groups were called sub-castes. For example in Maharashtra there are about a dozen castes which are engaged in making all kinds of earthen pots. The maker of earthen pots is called Kumbhar (from Sanskrit *kumbha* — a pot and *kāra* — a maker). According to the older way of designation, each of the Kumbhar castes was called a sub-caste, while the caste-cluster of earthen pot-makers was called the

"Kumbhar caste". This mode of naming the smallest endogamous groups created the impression that sub-castes were smaller groups derived through the sub-division of an entity called caste. A few examples were known of a split within a caste leading to the establishment of two new separate endogamous units; but such cases are exceptions rather than the rule.

Names of castes within a caste-cluster also helped to strengthen this impression. There are the following names by which the endogamous castes within the caste-cluster Kumbhar are known. The word Kumbhar is common to all these appellations and to it are prefixed other words. They are : Thor-chake Kumbhar (big-wheel Kumbhar), Lahan-chake Kumbhar (small-wheel Kumbhar), Kurere Kumbhar (stone-slab Kumbhar), Hat-ghade Kumbhar (shaping-pots-with-hands Kumbhar), Gadheria Kumbhar (donkey-using Kumbhar), etc. It was never expressly stated that an original Kumbhar caste split into various endogamous units owing to some people coming to use different implements and techniques or owing to the use of certain animals like donkeys for carrying the pots, but the way in which the whole caste system was described gave this impression.

Anthropologists were aware of the fact that some of the units called sub-castes had their origin from primitive people, some from some immigrant tribes, but the way the castes were described led to the belief that they arose through the splitting of an original entity in two ways, firstly through occupational specialisation in a casteless society and secondly through further specialisation, which led to further splitting of bigger groups. Also when caste was described as a social organization, the description and analysis made mention of castes bearing the same or similar names over very wide areas including many linguistic regions, sometimes over the whole of India and the impression was strengthened that either (1) the castes bearing similar names were products of fission of an original single body or that (2) each linguistic region having a single

casteless society split into several endogamous groups called castes.

This way of dealing with castes, together with the use
of words like fission, segmentation or fragmentation was
based on the theory that the castes are a product of continuous fragmentation. The following passage from
Professor GHURYE's book[9] suggests that sub-castes arose
out of castes. "A close study of the name of the various
minor units, the so called sub-castes, within the major
groups reveals the fact that the bases of distinction *leading to the exclusive marking off* of these groups were
territorial separateness, mixed origins, occupational distinction, some peculiarity in the technique of one and the
same occupation, sectarian differences, dissimilarity of
customs ...." (italics mine).

The history and origin of caste was envisaged in the
following way[10] :—

An early period, roughly corresponding to the Vedic
period, in which one finds mention of three *varṇas* but not
of *jāti*, then a period of four *varṇas*, then a period of
numerous *jātis* with untouchability coming in and a final
period of fossilisation of the fragmented society divided
into innumerable small castes. The Indian village was
depicted as the point where castes came together to form
a common society based on mutual support and specialisation of function.

Professor GHURYE states that caste was based on the
attempts by the Brahmins to keep their racial purity. He
makes a guess at the physical characteristics of the early
Aryan settlers, tries to show that those characteristics are
best preserved in all castes of the Punjab and in the Brahmin and Khatri castes of Uttar Pradesh and that as one
goes down the ladder of caste hierarchy, the characteris-

[9] Professor G. S. GHURYE first clearly enunciated this theory in his
book *Caste and Race in India*, 1932, (3rd edition published in
1957 under the name *Caste and Class in India*, Bombay.) It was
implicit in the work of Indologists and of RISLEY, which is quoted
by Professor GHURYE.

[10] Loc. cit.

tics of the population are the farthest removed from those of the hypothetical Aryans. The existence of separate castes in the "homogeneous" population of the Punjab is then presumably due to segmentation or fission as a result of intermingling with the aboriginal population and specialisation of occupation. He writes, "The idea of endogamy and other elements of caste were taken by Brahmin prospectors with them (all over India)". (*loc. cit.* Chap. 7). They could not influence the racial composition of the other regions as they did in the north of India, the land of their original colonisation, but they did "try to apply their scheme of occupational segregation and endogamy to various groups *according to their receptive abilities*" (italics mine). "This racial origin of the principal feature of the caste system is further supported by the early term *varṇa* meaning colour used to specify the orders in society." .... "I may conclude that caste in India is a Brahmanic child of the Indo-Aryan culture, cradled in the land of the Ganga and the Yamuna and thence transferred to the other parts of the country." ((*loc. cit.* Chap. 7, pp. 178-179). He further says, "The lack of rigid unitary control of the State, the unwillingness of the rulers to enforce a uniform standard of law and custom, their readiness to recognise the varying customs of different groups as valid, and their usual practice of allowing things somehow to adjust themselves helped the *fissiparous* (italics mine) tendency of groups and fostered the spirit of solidarity and community feeling in every group." (p. 182).

Professor GHURYE then adds, "Multiplicity of the groups and the thoroughness of the whole system are due to the habit of the Hindu mind to create categories and carry things to their logical end ...." To this sentence is added a foot-note : "Prof. C. G. SELIGMAN attributes this mental trait to the Nordic race. (See his presidential address to the Royal Anthropological Institute, *J.R.I.A.*, 1924)". Professor GHURYE obviously wishes to imply that the Indian Aryans were a branch of the Nordic (?) race.

This has been the classical picture of the Hindu society as presented by modern anthropologists. I also worked on these assumptions, but every year I became more and more dissatisfied with this formulation, because it did not tally with my experience. While parts of the description were accurate, the total formulation was not satisfactory and so I am stating here what appears to me to be the true orientation towards caste. This orientation makes caste an aspect of the total picture of the Hindu culture through the ages — not an ingenious creation of the Brahmins, but a thing which has been there perhaps even before the Brahmins came on the scene. The Brahmins attempted to understand it, account for it, make use of it, but do not seem to be its creators. They were as much creatures of it as the other castes. I wish to place the phenomenon of caste as part of the total cultural process. Many anthropologists have described caste. I do not therefore wish to describe it in detail but it is necessary to stress certain aspects in order to understand its role in providing the variety of behavioural pattern to which attention has been drawn.

II

THE NATURE OF THE GROUP CASTE

I have designated caste as the carrier and the preserver of the variety which characterises Hindu society. Though most of the attributes of caste have been well described by other anthropologists, I shall describe a few characteristics, which will be referred to in this book again and again.

In order to understand properly what a caste is, it would be better to describe castes in one area first instead of for the whole of India. I am restricting myself to the linguistic area of Maharashtra primarily and then for illustrating certain points I shall consider castes from other areas.

(a) Castes are endogamous groups;

(b) castes are restricted to certain limited areas;

(c)   castes have a certain tradional behaviour pattern
which is enforced in many cases by a "caste council"
made up of a number of respected elder men in a
caste;

(d)   castes live together with other castes without mingling except on certain occasions only. The intercourse between castes is peripheral or tangential;

(e)   a caste has generally a hereditary occupation, which
is however not exclusive to it;

(f)   castes are arranged in a hierarchical order.

Let us consider the above points one by one.

A caste is an endogamous group. The endogamy of a
caste is broken in two ways. The first is a legal marriage
between a man of a higher caste to a woman of a lower
caste. This is called hypergamy and is found in certain
parts of India among only certain castes and is not a general practice in any region. The second exception to endogamy is an exception in a biological sense. Marriage
involves certain duties and rights and status for the progeny. In this respect caste-endogamy can be termed almost universal except for the few hypergamous practices.
The second exception, while leading to sexual relations
across caste, has little effect on the family organization
or the caste organization as such. In this category are
to be mentioned practices of concubinage, housemaids and
prostitution. Very young girls were bought as concubines
and lived as secondary wives with the man who bought
them. The man was called "master" (*malik*) by the concubine. The practice was not uncommon some twenty-five
years ago. A man may take as concubine a widow from
a lower caste. These two relationships were quite open.
Men also had more or less permanent relations with some
women in a less open way. Landed gentry and men from
aristocratic or ruling families had free access to the maids
of their wives. The author has seen a will, which made
provision for such a "maid" and her progeny. Such maids
and their progeny have become a separate caste in Rajputana. The males are called *khavās* and the females

khavāsin. In every princely Rajput marriage the bride was accompanied by elderly and young *khavāsins* from her father's house, the former as advisers of the bride and the latter as concubines for the husband.

The prostitutes always formed a recognized part of the society. They were generally drawn from the lower castes. Various social workers have noted that Mahar women made up a large section of the prostitutes in the city of Bombay. Mahar women were also used by the British army. A special class of "protected" women was formed by singers and dancers of high repute who were and are concubines to and under the protection of a rich patron. The progeny of these formed part of the mother's caste.

As regards the spread of a caste and its being confined generally to a linguistic region, it may be noted that border groups in many cases are bilingual and retain kinship ties across linguistic frontiers; but elsewhere a caste used to be confined to the linguistic area. A caste, because of its endogamy, was described by me as an extended kinship group.[11] In an extended kinship group all people can be shown to be related to one another either by affinal or by agnatic ties. Two people need not be related directly as agnates or as affines, but they may both be related to a third person with whom one is an agnate and the other is an affine.

Two attempts were made in this respect, which indicate the probable validity of the above statement in the case of two castes, one numbering about 200,000 and the other about 250,000. The first caste is that of the Chitpavan Brahmins. They have family names and about 150 distinct family names are known. Families having the same name trace their descent from a common ancestor, not merely theoretically, but in most cases actually. In this community, marriage among close kin and exchange marriages are not allowed. It was thought that if one

[11] *Society in India*, Ed. by A. AIYAPPAN and L. K. BALARATNAM, Social Science Association, Museum House, Madras, 1956, pp. 29-48.

chose a big family and recorded all the marriages for some
generations one may be able to get all the 150 names of the
families among the kin group. This investigation is still
in progress, but the preliminary results do tend to show
such connections. The family chosen was that of
"Ranade" in Poona. Upto now only a portion of the
Poona family has been covered where the marriages are
recorded of all the "Ranade" descendants of one Ram-
chandra Ranade, who lived in and near Poona in the 19th
century. According to this bit of genealogy, 98 Ranade
men and women have married into 60 separate families
which is 40 per cent of all the Chitpavan family names.
In this genealogy only the spouses of Ranade-born people
have been recorded. When we include the marriages of
the descendants of women born as Ranade but given into
other families as brides, we can most probably get all the
names of the Chitpavan families.

The second attempt was made while investigating the
marriage practices of the "Gangadikar Vokkaliga", an
agricultural caste of Mysore. This caste is spread over
four districts of Mysore and is divided into exogamous
clans. The people of this caste practise cross-cousin
marriage. Three villages at three different localities in
their territory of occupation were chosen. Within each
village containing numerous families belonging to different
exogamous clans every one was related to every one else
by ties of marriage and/or blood and between the three
villages there were a few families who were directly related so that even the most distant Gangadikar Vokkaligas
could be shown to be bound by kinship ties.[12] Similar in-

---

[12] The rules of marriage of these two castes — the Chitpavan and
the Gangadikar Vokkaliga — are a little more complicated than
stated here, especially the regulations about the avoidance of
Gotra; but the outline given here suffices for the point I am illustrating. The investigation on the Gangadikar Vokkaliga was
carried out by Mrs. Bhavani BANERJEE and is incorporated in the
thesis for Ph.D., University of Poona, 1959, entitled "Marriage
and Kinship of the Gangadikar Vokkaligas of Mysore". The
Deccan College Research Institute is publishing the thesis.

vestigations need to be undertaken for some of the northern castes, which do not possess family names or exogamous clans with totemic symbols and which practise village exogamy.

Most of the Indian castes, i.e. endogamous groups, are within the 200,000 limit as regards numbers. There are a few bigger groups like the Marathas in Maharashtra (the population is over 5,000,000) and the Rajputs in Rajasthan. These groups show a very elaborate structure of hypergamy and seem to represent fusion of separate tribal elements. The rule of endogamy may hold true as regards these castes, but it would be difficult to prove the proposition about kinship. The task of investigation is not too difficult as both these castes are divided into exogamous patrilineal clans.

The various endogamous groups are not products of fission, but seem to have been independent and of different origin. Below are described a number of castes belonging to different caste-clusters in Maharashtra, which are known respectively under the names of (i) Maratha-Kunbi, (ii) Brahmin, (iii) Kumbhar, and (iv) Mahar.

This description will show how each caste within a caste-cluster differs from the other castes in its traditions and the region it occupies. The Maratha-Kunbi caste-cluster comprises castes engaged in agriculture; the Brahmin caste-cluster is made up of castes whose hereditary occupation is priest-craft, but who also own land and lend money; the Kumbhar are representative of an artisan caste-cluster and lastly the Mahars represent the castes whose touch or even shadow was supposed to pollute others.

I have chosen the Maratha-Kunbi caste-cluster as representing the land-owning and land-tilling castes. The word "Kunbi" is applied to various groups of tillers of land. The word "Maratha" used to be applied to a particular group in western Maharashtra. In successive censuses of India the word Kunbi has receded until at last in the latest census which mentioned any caste at all (the 1941 census), the word has all but vanished. Gradually all Kunbis have given their caste either as Maratha or as some kind of Kshatriya.

The Maratha-Kunbi form over 40 per cent of the population of western Maharashtra. Of these the Marathas consider themselves as rulers and aristocrats and do not marry the Kunbis. Measurements have failed to show any difference between the Maratha and the Kunbi. Among themselves they show less variation than the Brahmins do.[13] The Kunbi-Marathas of the plateau of western Maharashtra seem to belong to a great wave of immigration of a meso- to sub-brachy-cephalic people possessing cattle and practising agriculture, which started from somewhere in north Gujarat and ended in Coorg.[14]

The accounts about castes other than Brahmins cannot be as detailed as those of the Brahmins because the inscriptional records do not contain names of the present clans and the Kshatriyas of old cannot be identified certainly with the present Marathas, though there is no doubt that some names of the present clans are those of the old ruling dynasties.

The Marathas of the districts of Poona, Satara, Kolhapur, Ahmednagar, parts of Khandesh and Sholapur marry among themselves. All these people worshipped the god Shiva, Khandoba and Bhavani (the mother goddess) besides a number of minor deities. The preferred type of marriage is that of a man to his mother's brother's daughter. The marriage of a man to his father's sister's daughter is tabooed. The women of the higher status rarely went out of the house. These people were excellent dry farmers and guerrilla fighters, who struggled for twenty-five years with the Moghul power and drove it out of their land.

---

[13] In a recent personal communication, this finding was confirmed through blood-grouping by Dr. V. R. Khanolkar of the Tata Cancer Research Institute, Bombay.

[14] KARVE and DANDEKAR, *Anthropometric Measurements of Maharashtra*, Deccan College Monograph Series, Poona, 1951. Pp. 49-65 and 81-83.

There was another group of poorer landholders, who used to be called Kunbi in the same area of the high plateau, which seems to have merged with the Maratha group. The Kunbi living in the western coastal strip (Konkan) is an endogamous group and never marries outside of that group. The family names of these people are entirely different from those of the Marathas and Kunbis of the plateau. They worship local gods, though some visit the shrine of Vithoba in Pandharpur. Their forms of worship are different from those of the Marathas. The Kunbi women work in the rice fields with their men. In physical build they are different from the Marathas. Among them also a man may marry his mother's brother's daughter, but not his father's sister's daughter.

In parts of Khandesh and Berar are people who call themselves Leva or Leva Kunbi. They are different in their dress, speech and appearance from both the above groups. They are dolicho-cephals (cephalic index : 74) unlike the western Kunbis and Marathas (cephalic index : 77-79). Their area of occupation on both sides of the Barhanpur gap suggests that they are recent immigrants from the north. Their name may point to affinities to the Leva Kunbi of Gujarat, but the social organization of the two groups differs in many significant details. The Khandesh Levas practise the marriage of a man to his mother's brother's daughter. They have no traditions of fighting. They are an extremely industrious group and their women follow the milk trade. They tend buffaloes and sell milk and milk products. This activity again connects them with the north. Neither the Marathas nor the Kunbis of the plateau or Konkan are good pastorals, though the Marathas take good care of their draught bullocks.

In Berar and Nagpur the dominant Kunbi group is called Tirole Kunbi. They differ from the western Kunbis in many respects. Their heads are narrower than the Marathas. Unlike the Marathas and western Kunbis they allowed the re-marriage of a widow to the younger brother of the husband and they did not formerly lay claim to be fighters.

From among the numerous other castes calling themselves Kunbis only one need be mentioned. This is called Mana or Manwa Kunbi. They are found in the Chanda and Yeotmal districts. Some castes are not willing to grant Kunbihood to the Manas. They seem to be a semi-primitive people living on the borders of Telangana and Maharashtra, who have taken the appellation Kunbi in recent years. Their cephalic and nasal indices and circumference of head place them nearer to the primitives than to the other castes.

Similar variety is found also among the Brahmin caste-cluster of Maharashtra. As an example I have chosen only a few major groups among the Brahmins, viz. Saraswat, Karhade, Chitpavan, Deshastha Ṛgvedi, Madhyandina and Charak.

The Saraswat Brahmins of Maharashtra[15] belong to the western coastal region between Malwan and Mangalore. All the families of the Saraswat which live today to the south (as far as Cochin), north (as far as Bombay), or south east (as far as Madras) of this region, can be shown to have their home within the region stated above.

Unlike other Brahmins of the south they eat fish. They speak a language which is held by some authorities to be an independent language and not a dialect of Marathi. In India they are the southernmost people speaking a Sanskritic language. Their deities are the mother goddess in her auspicious forms, and the god Shiva called Mangesh. In this caste a man can marry his mother's brother's daughter. Other types of marriage are allowed under exceptional circumstances.[16]

---

[15] There are other Brahmin castes calling themselves Saraswat Brahmins in other linguistic regions of India.

[16] In the case of exchange marriage (called (*Satelote* in Marathi) a man can marry his father's sister's daughter. Ordinarily such a marriage is not allowed. I have also recorded a case of a man marrying his "elder sister's daughter", but this is also not the usual Southern Indian type of marriage inasmuch as the "elder sister's daughter" in this case is so only by status and not a "blood relation". See genealogies in *Kinship Terminology and Usages of the Maratha Country*, BULL. DCRI, Vol. 2, Nos. 1 and 2, p. 21, Poona, 1940.

Epigraphic records show that they have been occupying the coastal strip and the neighbouring places on the mountains at least since the Kadamba dynasty, i.e. since the 12th century. Anthropometric measurements show them to be one among the three broad-headed communities of Maharashtra. They are followers of the Rgveda school of ritual.

The Karhade Brahmins are immediately to the north of the Saraswats and occupy an extremely restricted area. Historical records show that they had a settlement near the town of Karhad on the western edge of the Deccan plateau in the 12th century. They seem to have been an important community holding revenue offices during the period between the 10th and 13th centuries. They also preferred the marriage of a man to his mother's brother's daughter, but also allowed the marriage of a man to his sister's daughter and to his father's sister's daughter. Traditionally they are strict vegetarians. They are the followers of the Rgvedic branch of ritual. They worship the mother goddess. There was a belief among certain communities in Maharashtra that the Karhadas sometimes offered human sacrifice to their goddess. There are records of this belief but not a single authentic case of such a performance. It would appear that they were originally a community of Brahmins living on the Deccan plateau but migrated to the coast *en masse* some time during the 12th or 13th century. Anthropometric measurements show that they possess the longest heads (absolute measurements) of all the Maharashtra communities. They also have the largest circumference of the head.

The Chitpavan Brahmins occupy the land north of the Karhadas. There do not seem to be as old records about this community as about the other Brahmin communities of Maharashtra. They seem to have started a migration to the high plateau of the Deccan a little before Shivaji's times (17th century). The migration has continued right upto the present century. This caste has within it some families which follow the rituals according to the Krishna Yajurveda, while there are others which follow some

branch of R̥gvedic rituals. The author believes that they
are unique in this feature as all the other major Brahmin
castes of Maharashtra follow one Veda only. They do not
allow marriage among any type of near kin.[17] Their main
deity seems to be the god Shiva whose shrines ending with
the syllables "Ishwara" are found along the coastal strip
occupied by them.[18] A female goddess, merely called Devi
(i.e. Goddess) always accompanies the more specifically
mentioned male god, e.g. "the Ishwara of such and such
shrine and Devi." Thus a particular family would have
the Vyaghreshwar of Asud village and Devi as their
deities. Like all southern Brahmins they do not eat fish
or meat. They have head breadth and head length smaller
than either the Saraswats or the Karhadas. They are
mesocephalic. All Brahmins of the coast are generally
fairer than those of the plateau. The Chitpavans distinguish themselves in having a larger percentage of hazel
or cats' eyes than the other coastal communities (over 10
per cent.)

The other three Brahmin communities live on the
Deccan plateau called "Desh". The Deshastha R̥gvedi
Brahmins, as their name suggests, live in the Desh and
follow a R̥gvedic ritual. They are an extremely widespread and numerous community. They worship different
deities, but quite a large number have Khandoba as their
family god. Many of them are hereditary worshippers of
the Vithoba of Pandhapur. The marriage of a man to his
mother's brother's daughter is the one considered orthodox.
A man's marriage to his elder sister's daughter is also
found among them and rarely also a man's marriage to his
father's sister's daughter. This caste is found in western
and central Deccan along the banks of the Godavari and
the Krishna and has spread deep into Karnatak. There
are frequent inter-marriages between Karnatak and Maharashtra families in this community. They appear to be
the oldest Brahmin community of this region belonging

---

[17] The author has recorded a few exception to this rule.
[18] Velneshwar, Koleshwar, Vyaghreshwar are some of the shrines.

perhaps to a period when parts of Maharashtra, Karnatak and Telangana formed a mighty kingdom under the dynasties of Chalukya, Rashtrakuta and Yadava.

The Madhyandina Brahmins are also a large community. They are found predominantly in northern and central Maharashtra and share the Godavari towns with the Rgvedis. They have many peculiarities which distinguish them from the other Brahmins.

(i) They represent not one Veda, but a sub-school of a Veda. The Vedic school called the Shukla Yajurveda is itself the latest among all Vedic schools and the fact of a caste based on a sub-school of a late Veda makes one feel that they are rather a late accession to Brahminhood. In Sanskrit literature they are mentioned as the Brahmins par excellence of the Kaliyuga.

(ii) Unlike the Saraswat and Rgvedi Deshastha Brahmins, they avoid not only all kin-marriage, but forbid the marriage of a man into the Gotra of his mother even when there is no kinship relation.

This regulation is followed by many castes of northern India and the author would take this trait as a sign of the late immigration of these Brahmins from the north. This is supported by the fact that the Brahmins of this sub-school are almost unknown to the south of the Krishna river. THURSTON remarks that in the south these Brahmins are supposed to attain Brahminhood only after midday. Madhyandina means "of the midday"; it is also the name of a person, a pupil of Yajnyavalkya, the founder of Shukla Yajurveda and followers of Madhyandina are known by his name. Apparently the name was misunderstood or deliberately misinterpreted by the southern Brahmins.

There are many family gods among this caste. Quite a number of families in eastern Maharashtra are worshippers of the mother goddess Renuka of Mahurgad. The anthropometric measurements come nearest to those of the Maratha caste (cephalic index : 76.1 to 80.2). Most of the people are dark, but some are extremely fair.

The Charak Brahmins are a tiny community found in the district of Nagpur. They belong to the Charak school of Krishna Yajurveda. Unlike the other Brahmins, they possess rather small heads. Both breadth and length are small (cephalic index : 79.16; circumference of head smallest among Brahmins, 532 mm.)

The Kumbhar caste-cluster is chosen as representing an artisan caste-cluster. From west to east in Maharashtra there are a dozen castes making pottery. Each is endogamous, each goes by a specific name and each has slightly different ways of making pots or has some other peculiarities exclusive to itself.

The Maratha Kumbhar are spread all over the western plateau. Among them there are people who make only hand-made pottery, some specialize in making roof tiles, some make bricks and some turn big and small pots on wheels. I found family-wise specialization. I also found in some cases one brother turning water pots while the other made huge pottery containers called *kundis* for garden plants. Our records show free marriage among all these families. They practise both types of cross-cousin marriage but no uncle-niece marriage. Unlike the Marathas and the Kunbis they do not have clans or clan names. All Kumbhars of a village are called after the village and do not intermarry, e.g. the 'Supekar' are from the village of Supe. This feature is northern Indian. These Kumbhars however have no memory of having come into Maharashtra from any land or region outside Maharashtra.

In Poona there are Kumbhars called "Pardeshi Kumbhar", who are new immigrants from the north as the name suggests (Pardesh = Other country). They are an endogamous caste and do not marry with the Maratha Kumbhars. They specialize in making clay figurines either by free hand modelling or by using moulds.

To the east of Poona district is found a Marathi speaking Kumbhar caste, which calls itself Lingayat Kumbhar. They are divided into clans, practise clan exogamy and belong to the Lingayat sect of Shiva worshippers. Our blood-group investigation shows that unlike Maratha and Pardeshi Kumbhars some of them possess sickle cells.

In the Khandesh district of northern Maharashtra are two endogamous Kumbhar castes called respectively Thor-Chake (big-wheeled) and Lahan-Chake (small-wheeled). One uses a big wheel for turning the pots, the other a small wheel. The former are also called Lad Kumbhar. Lada or Lata is an ancient name for south Gujarat. These Kumbhars may be immigrants from the Lata region. The Lahan-Chake are also called Ahir Kumbhar. This shows that they believe that they have some connection with the Ahirs. Khandesh was once ruled over by Ahir or Abhir kings. The language of Khandesh is called the Ahirani dialect of Marathi. The Ahir language has many affinities to Gujarati. Many castes in Khandesh prefix the word Ahir to their caste name. Besides the Kumbhars there are the Ahir Sonars (goldsmiths). The Thor-Chake and Lahan-Chake thus differ not only in the fact of working with wheels of different sizes but in other respects also and are possibly of different origins.[19]

In West Khandesh there is yet another caste of Kumbhar called Hat-Ghade or Bhonkar, which is entirely endogamous. Its technique is also very peculiar. A man takes an old pot, places it with its mouth on the ground and pats clay on its upper surface, which is really the lower half. He smoothens the layer and dries the pot for some time in the sun and lifts the dried portion off. Then he places this half-made pot with its bottom down, takes fresh wet clay and shapes the upper portion with the gradually narrowing mouth. These water-pots are rather thick. The process in some way is analogous to that used by Bhil women in making their grain bins of clay. This Kumbhar caste seems to represent a tribal element.

In north-eastern Maharashtra there are many Kumbhar castes and each seems to be of a separate folk origin. Some (the Kurere, as they are called) use a stone slab

---

[19] Physical measurements and blood-group investigation of the Kumbhars is in progress.

turning on a pivot instead of a wheel. I understand that this technique is used by potter castes in the Gangetic plains. Quite a number of communities in this part of India are immigrants from the north. The Sungaria, another potter caste, who eat and keep pigs seem to be of primitive origin.

The Mahar is the name of a great "scheduled" caste of Maharashtra. But even among them there are small endogamous units. There appear to be a smaller number of such units in this group than among others. The Mahars of eastern Maharashtra do not marry those of western Maharashtra, nor those of the Konkan. It would therefore be better to call them a caste-cluster rather than one single caste. In each sub-region they follow the marriage practices of the predominant agricultural caste. Anthropologically they occupy a position halfway between the primitives and the other Hindus, somewhat nearer to the Hindus than to the primitives. They seem to belong to tribal elements very early drawn into the village economy of the Deccan. They are in intimate touch with primitive areas even now. The differences among them can be judged from the fact that while I found no sickle cells among the Mahars of western Maharashtra, Dr. SHUKLA of Nagpur in a personal communication reported sickling among Nagpur Mahars.

We thus find that the groups which practise endogamy are different from each other as regards their habits, cultural traits and, in many cases, ethnic and racial origins. To call them sub-castes and group them under other groups called castes does not seem to be justified in the face of these findings.[20]

Each caste is a self-contained group which cannot be put in a scheme of classification comprising broad groups, sub-groups within each group and sub-divisions within

---

[20] This does not deny that in a few cases castes may have arisen through split, but such cases must be authenticated. The "Dasā" and "Visā" castes in Gujarat, bearing otherwise the same name, indicate a certain ranking. Whether these divisions indicate products of split needs investigation.

each such sub-group similar to phyla, genus, class and sub-class as in botany and zoology. We can however understand the rationale of the older type of classification if we analyse the relationship of caste to occupation and of caste to rank.

Each caste has generally a traditional hereditary occupation. In the case of some castes there are injunctions against following occupations other than the traditional ones. A particular type of occupation is however never co-extensive with a single caste. Typically, several castes follow a single occupation. For example in the city of Poona there are several endogamous castes following the profession of goldsmiths : Ahir-Sonar, Lad-Sonar, Daivadnya-Sonar, etc. Among potters there are the Maratha Kumbhar, Pardeshi Kumbhar, Lad Kumbhar and Kachchi Kumbhar. In the same way there are various priestly castes called Brahmin. In the majority of cases the several castes which practise the same profession are known by hyphenated or double names, one part of which signifies the occupation and is the same for a whole set of castes. Thus in the names of the castes enumerated above the words Sonar (goldsmith), Kumbhar (potter) and Brahmin (priest) are common to several castes. In descriptive accounts of castes, whether in old and medieval Sanskrit and Prakrit literature or in modern anthropological literature, a majority of castes is given a name derived from their profession. In the late 19th and 20th century accounts (the various volumes of *Castes and Tribes* of different regions published in connection with the decennial censuses of India from 1881 onwards), one almost always finds the word Sonar as the name of "a caste". The various endogamous castes which practise this profession over one or more linguistic regions are referred to in English as subcastes. Actually I have argued that these are groups of castes following the same occupation, they are caste-clusters.

In any village if one asks casually about the different resident castes (*Jāti*), one normally gets as an answer only the occupation names, e.g. Sutar (carpenter), Lohar

(iron-smith), Koshti (weaver) and so on. If one asks
further about any particular caste then one gets the full
information about the particular endogamous unit to which
the local followers of the particular craft belong. It is this
phenomenon which is partly responsible for the introduction of the word sub-caste and deserves closer consideration.

Not all castes following the same occupation are known
by the same name denoting a caste-cluster. Kunbi is the
general name in Maharashtra for all types of agriculturists. The name is applied to owners of small farms,
tenants and also to farm workers. Tirole Kunbi are both
owners and tenants. Mana Kunbi are in most cases un-
free labourers on land. There are however a number of
castes which do the same type of work but have different
names probably denoting tribes. Such are the Andh of
eastern Maharashtra and the Warli and Agari of western
Maharashtra. In the case of these latter nobody has called them sub-castes of the Kunbi caste; they have always
been given the status of independent castes.

"Brahmin" is the name of priests who follow the ritual
according to certain Sanskritic rites. There are a host of
other priests belonging to special castes with different
names like Bhagat,[21] Gunia, Baria, Gurav, etc. Nobody
has called these sub-castes of some big priestly caste. They
have always been acknowledged for what they are : independent endogamous castes.

Another fact, which must be remembered is that the
existence of a number of endogamous castes following similar profession and called by the same name over a linguistic area or over the whole of India was, in the past, generally not known to the individuals belonging to the
separate castes. Each caste has its own area of extent in
which there is kinship and marriage, mutual visiting and

---

[21] Bhagats are found among many so-called lower castes, sometimes
as a special caste, sometimes as a family. Gunia are the priests
of some of the aborigines. Baria is the ruling priestly caste
among the semi-primitive Binzals of Orissa.

meetings of caste councils. At the periphery there is a certain overlap and people may know of another endogamous caste which follows the same occupation but which differs from their own in other patterns of behaviour. Within the area over which a caste is spread it is known simply by its occupation like Kumbhar (potter) or Chambhar (shoe-maker). In the contact area one caste differentiates itself from any other with a similar occupation. Only in the case of the knowledge of the existence of other similar castes is the necessity felt to differentiate one's own endogamous group from another. Near Mysore the term "Vokkaliga" is applied to Gangadikar Vokkaliga only and people belonging to that caste call themselves simply "Vokkaliga". But in north Karnatak, there are other Vokkaliga groups (castes), who know of each other's existence and always differentiate themselves as Kuda-Vokkaliga, and Sada-Vokkaliga. The latter in their region call themselves either Vokkaliga or Cadaru.

In an old document a village of the Konkan coast (western Maharashtra) is described.[22] In it are mentioned Brahmin, Kunbi and other castes. As the descendants of the people mentioned are still living in the village, their precise castes can be determined and the name of the particular Brahmin caste and Kunbi caste can be stated. But the writer of the document did not feel it necessary to mention any more specific caste names since the village contained only one caste each of Brahmins and Kunbis.

Before taking up the question of occupation and ranking, one feature deserves study. A caste is in some ways a cell-like structure which for many purposes is separated from other similar cells and lives a life partly independent of them. Caste society is made up in such a way that a very large proportion of the activity of the individuals is

---

[22] This document has been reproduced in part in the first chapter of the Marathi Autobiography of Dr. D. K. KARVE, *Atmavritta* by Dhondo Keshav KARVE, 1915. Another copy of the document was found and published in 1958. The author thinks that the document is as old as the 15th century.

confined to their own group.   This is especially true of the
social and cultural aspects of their life.

In the economic sphere the individuals and the group
as a whole come in contact with other groups.   Buying and
selling, serving in particular capacities and being paid or
served in return, are the ways in which castes come in contact with other groups.   In cultural and social behaviour
castes are never completely self-sufficient or isolated nor
is economic dependence complete in all cases.   The economic activities which involve interaction with other groups
are of two types.   One type involves rendering of certain
traditional services at traditional and generally inadequate
compensation and the other type can be described as
economic inter-dependence where mutual services and
compensations are more on terms of equality.   Whether
the economic activity is on equitable terms or whether it
is a traditional form of exploitation, it brings individuals
from one caste into contact with individuals from other
castes.   This quality of being comparatively self-contained
in social and cultural activities and at the same time being
linked with other groups in economic activities is a fundamental characteristic of the groups called castes.

A few examples will elucidate this.   A survey was
made two years ago to find out the nature and degree of
intercommunal activity in rural areas.[23]   For this work
three villages were chosen and the head of each family was
asked certain questions.   The habitation area and the
house sites were mapped.   The questions asked were :
Who had married · whom?   Who had given presents to
whom?   Whom did you invite for a meal?   For a less in-
formal party?   For a cup of tea?   By whom were you invited for such hospitality?   Whom did you visit for a few
days?   A day and night?   or for a few hours?   Who were
own friends?   the children's friends?   If casual help was
given, what was its nature and to whom was it given?   Who
was tenant to whom?   Who employed whom?   Who bor-

---

[23] This survey was undertaken at the Deccan College, Poona on
behalf of the Planning Commission.   It is awaiting publication.

rowed money from whom? In addition there were questions about attitudes to inter-group intercourse.

The picture that emerged when all the data were tabulated was that the habitation area in each village was divided into areas containing houses of one caste. Within each such area contiguous houses belonging to one patrilineage could be discovered as clusters. Besides the caste clusters the whole area was generally divided into two main habitation areas, one belonging to the higher castes, the touchables, and the other belonging to the lowest castes, the untouchables. Different castes among touchables and untouchables within these larger areas lived a little separated from the others. The village habitation area was thus roughly divided into as many units as there were castes in the village. (A few exceptions were those who did not own a house but lived in rented quarters).

In the three villages surveyed not a single marriage had occurred outside the caste. The attitudes showed that only one or two people among the higher castes expressed the opinion that they did not mind mixed marriages. As many as 25 to 50 per cent of the Mahars (one untouchable caste) expressed willingness to give their daughters to touchables or receive brides from touchables, but were not willing to enter into marriage relation with the Mang, another untouchable caste.[24]

---

[24] What is happening in urban and semi-urban areas can be gauged from the extract below :

A survey of marriages registered in Poona City and district during the years 1955 and 1956 showed that out of a total of 5895 Hindu marriages 126 (2 per cent) were marriages between castes belonging to one caste-cluster. These were all marriages between different Brahmin castes. The number of marriages between castes belonging to different caste-clusters (not necessarily to different *varṇas*) was 41 (0.6 per cent) and the marriages of Hindus with people of other religions were 32. All the other marriages were inside the endogamous caste. From these figures one might say that marriages across the caste-clusters and *varṇa* were also as rare as marriages out of one's religion. The higher incidence of marriages within the caste-cluster called Brahmin need not be accepted as evidence of a continuation of

As regards inviting people to a meal, going to others for a meal and visiting for a few days, the activities were confined in nearly 90 per cent of cases to the kinship group. The remaining 10 per cent were within the caste group. The same was the case with friendships. Dr. McKim MARRIOTT of the University of Chicago, in a personal communication told the author that in his observation in north Indian villages also, friendships outside the caste group were not only rare, but were generally accompanied by much shame and feelings of guilt. Gift-giving, where the pattern is not disturbed by modern business relations, is confined almost purely to the kin group.

Giving and receiving of help include activities ranging from giving food grains to a man in need, to giving shelter in one's own house to somebody whose house had been burned down or nursing in illness. It was found that outright giving of food grains or clothing to people of a caste other than one's own was not uncommon but not a single case of sheltering in one's own house or of nursing an ill person of a caste other than one's own was recorded. A few people who had occasion to receive such help always did so from their kin or, on a few rare occasions, from unrelated people of their caste.

As regards the other activities, people were tenants to people of other castes, they borrowed money from any caste and accepted employment from anybody.

Thus purely social activities were confined within the caste, while economic activities cut across the caste

a supposed solidarity or homogeneity in the Brahmin *varṇa*. The Brahmins are the most educated castes of Maharashtra. They have been advocating social reforms and especially inter-Brahmin-cluster marriages for a long time and the anti-Brahmin movements of the past fifty years have made them aware of a common destiny. These events in recent history can explain the higher incidence of such marriages. It may be noted that of the 41 marriages of people of different caste-clusters, 28 were those in which one partner was a Brahmin.

This survey has been carried out by Mr. MOKASHI, a student of the Deccan College, Poona.

frontiers. On certain occasions in a village meals are
served to people of all castes. This does not form an exception to the above rule because the meals are not given
on terms of equality. Such meals are given only by the
richer and more influential people of the higher castes.
The near kin, the important people of one's own caste and
other people of higher castes sit for meals together. Such
people as the barber, the carpenter etc. may come into the
house and may be served meals in an open shed which is
part of the house, while people belonging to the untouchable castes may line the road outside and get their share of
food after everybody else has eaten. In all this context
a meal does not entail social give-and-take on terms of
equality.

The social self-containedness of the caste is broken on
certain occasions when all castes in a village appear to
combine for achieving certain common ends like celebrat-
ing certain festivals, sometimes for common defence
against dacoits and sometimes to make common representa-
tions to government. I have used the word 'sometimes'
deliberately, because the usual picture even of a dacoity is
that the poorer people either shut themselves up in their
houses or run away from the village and leave the richer
people to face the robbers. The poor and the rich are not
only economic classes but often caste groups too. Among
the Maratha and Brahmin groups there may be richer
and poorer people, but all of them are better off than the
Mahar, the Mang and the Ramoshi. In the same way the
few families belonging to the Vani caste are in possession
of more cash and ornaments than other castes.

The social isolation is broken more often in the modern urban setting. Boys of different castes study in the
same class and friendships are formed. These friendships
may remain outside of the family circle and may lead to
tensions and frustrations. Among people working in the
same place similar situations arise. As long as these
friendships are kept away from the family and the home,
there is no open conflict; but the minute they impinge on
that sphere tensions arise. This is especially the case

among people belonging to castes which are educationally and economically backward. If a man of such a caste tries to have a friendship with men of higher castes he is looked down upon as a climber by the advanced set, and earns hatred and jealousy from his own caste, who dub him a deserter.

The caste councils effectively control the behaviour of the members of the caste and punish abberrant practices. Castes thus have an agency of social control and punishment which is parallel to the agency of the state. Taking into consideration all these things a caste has been called "a state within a state and a kingdom within a kingdom". The castes thus have only peripheral or superficial contact with one another and though their isolation was not as complete as Leibnitzian Monads, it embraced many vital aspects of life.

A caste has generally a hereditary occupation, which however is not exclusive to it. People of one caste can follow different occupations. The choice in olden days was limited or in some cases denied by two considerations. The people of the lowest castes were not allowed to follow the occupations of the higher castes and people of the higher castes did not follow certain lowly occupations for fear of losing prestige or getting polluted. Barring these limiting circumstances there was some elasticity. If one studies the caste situation it will be evident that occupations needing special skills account for only a small number of people in the Indian population. There is specialization in the sense that food producers will only produce food and demand all the services from the other castes but the food producers account for the largest number of people in India. In Europe, in America and also among most primitive agriculturists in India there is quite a number of small jobs to which a farmer turns his hand. He may do some repair to his house and farm implements and some kind of carpentering, sometimes his women-folk will weave etc. But in many parts of India a farmer is just a farmer and nothing else.

Specialization of occupation can develop only in a society which can support workers who do not directly engage in activities for producing or procuring food. Such possibility arose for the first time in the history of mankind with the discovery of agriculture. In the cities of ancient civilizations specialists of all types followed their respective trades in the cities. We have from many sources written accounts and archaeological evidence which give a picture of the activities of these artisans and artists. To what extent the rural areas of these ancient civilizations harboured specialists we do not know. In many developed societies even today the actual cultivator continues to perform a wide variety of occupations within his own family. Extreme specialization within rural society appears to be a distinctive characteristic of India. In addition to the basic producers of food who are also specialists — the agriculturists, fisher-folk, cattle-raisers, shepherds, etc.— there are to be found in the villages other specialists like skilled artisans, purveyors of many types of services, landlords and merchants.

Let us take a village in Maharashtra as an example. The majority of the households, say from 60 to 70 per cent, have as their main occupation agriculture. Some cultivators are landowners, some tenants. There are always one or two houses of shopkeepers. Then there are shoemakers, drummers, a butcher, a temple-servant, some shepherds, some Ramoshi (semi-tribal brigands), some carpenters. A few people come every year after the rains, live in the village for a few days, amuse the villagers with songs, dances, performances with tame animals or mend their metal pots and pans and collect grain in return. Many of the artisans own a little land, but let it out to tenants for cultivation. The landowning people and the tenants pay in kind every day as well as once a year to about seven or eight households for specific services rendered. These services consist of shaving, supplying ropes, repairing ploughs or making new ploughs, supplying earthen pots, playing music and dancing before the goddess at a festival, supplying iron implements like ploughshares, axes, etc. or repairing them, making new footwear and repairing them, officiating at rituals, servings as village accountant and scribe, and lastly, lowly offices such as removing dead cattle from the village habitation area or acting as messenger, village crier and watchman. For many other services, especially those of the professional reciter and dancer at the festival of the goddess, some money also has to be paid. Only the richer villages have a goldsmith. Nowadays he is generally found in the market towns. He is paid in cash and may be invited for meals at the houses of clients of higher castes.

Most of the transactions are still on the basis of exchange, inasmuch as services are paid for by cooked food or corn. The shop-keeper is in quite a different category from the other purveyors of goods and services. He supplies the ever indigent agriculturists whatever they need on the basis of deferred payment and almost always gets far more in money and kind than the goods supplied should cost. He is relatively well off and typically lends money to the cultivators.

If we look at this picture from the point of view of specialization, we find that specialization in the sense of possessing a learnt skill is found only in the case of the artisans. A carpenter, a goldsmith or a potter is a specialist. Some of the lower village services like working as a messenger or a sweeper are not at all specialised jobs requiring the acquisition of skills. In the same way among agriculturists the owners of land who get the land tilled in the traditional way through tenants cannot be called specialists. Other agriculturists do very hard and monotonous work which can be termed unskilled or semi-skilled heavy labour rather than specialization. Most of the menial services are also in the same category. Trading in the sense of shopkeeping, buying and selling again is not a special skill, except in so far as some amount of literacy and knowledge of account-keeping is required. Apart from the artisans, some of the persons providing priestly services can also be entitled specialists. Fisher-folk and boatmen are also specialists but not the drivers of bullock carts. We can say very roughly that not more than 15 per cent of the rural population is engaged in work needing some kind of special skills and all the rest possess no particular skills. The non-specialist majority consists of landlords and merchants on the one hand, and on the other, of actual farmers of all types whose work is hard and backbreaking but does not require special skill and people engaged in menial services other than farming.

What relation does the caste structure of the village bear to this occupational structure? As we might expect, the relation between caste and occupation is closest in the case of the relatively small group of occupational specialists. Common caste designations referring to occupations are, in fact, typical only of caste-clusters among the skilled artisans. Among the agriculturists the castes and caste-clusters have more often retained separate names reminiscent of tribal or other origins, which give no clue to the occupation followed. There will practically never be more than one caste of endogamous potters, carpenters or weavers within a village. But two or more quite distinct agricultural castes with totally unrelated names are very frequently settled in the same area and the same villages.

In the same way some of the castes doing menial jobs, agricultural labour, removing dead cattle, etc. have names which are neither common from region to region nor describe the type of work done. Such names are : Dhed, Mala, Madiga, Holeya, Mahar, Dom, Pana. In Maharashtra Maratha, Andh and Mana are agriculturists whose names tell us nothing of their occupations. On the other hand, Sonar (goldsmith), Lohar (ironsmith), Sutar (carpenter), are names of caste-clusters, which at once reveal the common occupation followed by all castes within the cluster.

To what extent do the members of the specialized and unspecialized castes actually follow the occupations which are carried in their caste names or considered traditional to their castes? Among Brahmins we have many instances in previous centuries as well as the present of individuals following vocations other than that of priesthood.

A Brahmin born in 1858 records in his autobiography that his grandfather was a wealthy trader who had lent a large sum of money to the ruling chief of Baroda.[25]   The Naik family, a Brahmin family of Baramati in Poona District were money-lenders by occupation in the 18th century. The Madhyandina Shukla Yajurvedi Brahmins of Maharashtra were well-known traders and money-lenders in pre-British times; the commerce of the whole of eastern Maharashtra was in their hands. People belonging to Brahmin castes have been rulers at various times and in various parts of India.[26]   A number of Brahmin castes have been traditionally landowners and remain so today. Many Brahmins served as government servants in the revenue department of the Mughal Kings.

King Harsha belonged to the Vaishya caste, who are supposed to be traders by profession. The Kayastha, who as a caste of scribes, were dismissed contemptuously in a Sanskrit drama (*Mudrarakshasa*), as of no importance, succeeded in establishing a dynasty in Bengal.[27]

As in other places in the world status depends upon a number of things like economic condition, birth, age, possession and conspicuous manifestation of certain qualities valued by society like learning, valour or saintliness, literary and artistic ability and power.

Status rarely depends on any one of these things, nor is there ever complete accord as regards a scale of values for the attributes enumerated above. Status is not just a value system in the abstract, but a value which receives concrete manifestation on innumerable occasions. A man may receive public recognition as citizen number one on a certain occasion but may be way down in the scale in the same society on certain other occasions. For example, in India, the older people always take precedence over the younger; the younger ones bow to the feet of the older

---

[25] *Atmavritta* by Dhondo Keshav KARVE, referred to above.

[26] Narmadeshwar PRASAD, *The Myth of the Caste-system*, pp. 68, 72, 80, etc.

[27] BASHAM, *The Wonder That Was India*, Grove Press, Inc., New York, 1954, p. 1, footnote; p. 47.

people and this normal procedure is reversed only on one occasion. The groom and the bride symbolise Vishnu and Laxmi, the god and goddess of prosperity, and the parents for once bow before their own child immediately after marriage. The man in power, whether king, minister or dictator, may pay homage publicly and bow his head before an acknowledged saintly man, but otherwise completely disregard his admonitions.

A society has almost never a fixed system of values in which the social concept of status can be determined rigidly. Under certain historical circumstances, status may attain both clarity and fixity in certain respects. Thus during the days of the British rule in India, the status of a Britisher was always higher than that of an Indian, whatever the status might have been in his own social structure. This order of importance remained even when the Hindu Brahmin thought he was polluted by the touch of the Britisher. An equally rigid definition of status has been in existence "theoretically" in India for centuries. Though this does not apply in its entirety to the present Indian situation, the value system of the structure has great effect on the thought, aspirations and actions of different castes; and to acquire full knowledge of the present tensions, it is necessary to describe in short this traditional scheme of status.

In Sanskrit and the modern Indian languages, this scheme is called "the four-rank system" (*Chaturvarna-samsthā*). The word "*varṇa*" has been taken by jurists, anthropologists and indologists to mean class, which is correct. It is used in grammar to denote a class of speech sounds. In this grammatical context *varṇa* means class but has no connotation of rank. However in the social system called the *varṇa* system, the idea of rank predominates and so in order to avoid misunderstandings arising out of the use of the word "class", which is used widely for a different type of social system in Western society, and to bring out clearly the underlying idea of status, the word "rank" has been used to denote *varṇa*.

This four-rank system has been very clearly described by Manu, who is supposed to be the first codifier of India. All other versions are expansions or modifications of the system as given by Manu. The version of Manu is given below in short.

Manu says, *jāti* are many while *varṇa* are only four. The latter are : Brahmin, Kshatriya, Vaishya and Shudra in that order. The first three are *dwija* (twice-born), i.e. have the right of going through the ritual of the thread ceremony, while the fourth rank has no such right. All the numerous *jāti* were brought into this four-rank system. Manu's whole scheme will be discussed later. For the present we may note that according to Manu Brahmins rank-ed as first, but this was never conceded by the Kshatriyas. The ancient literature comprising the Upanishads, the two epics Mahabharata and Ramayana, and the Puranas have many records of mutual rivalry and defiance of these two *varṇas*. Brahmins being the literate class, have reiterated their claim to be the first but narrated events show that the claim was at best but precariously held by the Brahmins.

The classical scheme and its modification through the ages make fascinating study, but need not be expanded here as they are largely irrelevant to the present study. The four ranks and their names are however important in understanding the problem of caste and status in the present context and so are explained below very briefly.

A description of the position of caste and *varṇa* in Maharashtra will help one to understand what prevails in other regions of India also. Each region reveals a slight variation depending mainly on (a) the history of the region, (b) the power and numerical strength — which in the modern context are sometimes synonymous — of the different castes, and (c) the safeguards offered by the Constitution. Of these factors the historical one is very prominent in Maharashtra.

Maharashtra was under Muslim rule from the 14th century. As a ruling people, Muslims enjoyed the same type of precedence which the British did during their days of domination in this country. Within the Hindu society Manu's four-fold ranking system — modified in certain respects — involving certain rights and disabilities held sway, as can be seen from the available literature and political and revenue documents. Manu's system was modified in two respects. Almost all the castes with the exception of the Brahmin were denied the right of the thread ceremony and thus made into Shudras. Among the Shudras a sub-rank was in existence. This sub-rank was made up of certain castes whose touch (even their shadow) was held to be polluting — this was the untouchable rank. In literature people wrote about the age-old four-rank system, but in effect there were only two *varnas*, viz. Brahmin and Shudra and a third one was later added — the untouchables who however were a sub-rank of the Shudra-*varna*. In the 17th century Shivaji was born, a Maratha, belonging to the clan of Bhonsla. The hereditary title of Raja was bestowed on his family by the Muslim kings of Bijapur. He fought successfully against the Muslim rulers of the south and against the Mughal emperor Aurangzeb and was crowned King of Maharashtra. An account dated 1697 of the event runs as follows : "Gagabhat, the man proficient in Vedas hearing of the great deeds of the Raja [Shivaji] came to see him. He, the great Brahmin, thought that if Muslims could sit on a throne and become Padshah, why should not the Raja, who had defeated four Padshahs and possessed seventy-five thousand horse soldiers, also be crowned in a similar way. The Maratha Raja must become a crowned king. The Raja acquiesced in this. So he brought together influential and powerful people who also agreed with the idea. Then he searched after the pedigree of Shivaji and found out that he was a "pure Kshatriya" belonging to the great house of Shisodia. Then he thought that the sacrament of thread ceremony should be performed on Shivaji as was the custom of the northern Kshatriyas. So in a sacred place Shivaji had the thread ceremony performed on him and was made a pure Kshatriya and then crowned King in the year 1674."[28]

In this significant document we learn that, in spite of the title of Raja being enjoyed by certain families of the Maratha caste, the caste itself was not recognised as Kshatriya, nor did it go through a ceremony entitling it to be called *dwija*.   A search (?) revealed Shivaji to be of Rajput origin.   This seems to have been the usual role of Brahmins who raised in this way many Shudra families to Kshatriyahood.   The thread ceremony had to be performed first and it may be noted that the Raja was 44 years old at the time it was performed.   (Generally it is performed before a boy is 12).

So a particular caste in western Maharashtra, till then supposed to be Shudra, became Kshatriya, and in the society of Maharashtra three *varṇas* were established.   There was no Vaishya *varṇa*, whose hereditary occupation was trade and shopkeeping.   The poet Tukaram, a contemporary of Shivaji was Maratha-Wani by caste.   He called himself Kunbi, i.e. a caste-group belonging to the Shudra *varṇa*.   This system continued upto the British period. After the British were well established, they started recording castes of people and almost from the time the results of the first census were published people of different castes started complaining that their caste name was wrongly described and that the real name was something else.   The "real" name always contained a claim to Brahminhood or Kshatriyahood by castes that were generally held to be Shudras.   Thus as late as in 1921, the Census Commissioner reported that the Daivadnya Sonar claimed to be Daivadnya Brahmin, that the Panchal Sutar claimed to be Vishwa Brahmin, the Jingar asserted that they should be described as Somavamshi Arya Kshatriya and Patwegars wanted to be called Somavamshi Sahasrarjuna Kshatriya.[29]

---

[28] *Sabhasada Bakhar*, written in 1697.   Edited and published by WAKASKAR at Baroda, 1957.
[29] *Census of India*, 1921, Vol. VIII, Part I, Appendix C, p. viii.

The present author had a similar experience when taking anthropometric measurements and blood groups of different castes. A caste near Bombay called Vadval (market gardeners) styled itself Somavamshi Kshatriya; another caste called Kalan claimed to be Dixit-Brahmin; a man from the Bhavsar caste enquired recently to find out whether it was true that the Bhavsar caste was reckoned as Shudra and not Kshatriya. Members of the Chandra-seniya Kayastha caste fought successfully with the Brahmins over this question and established their Kshatriya-hood by bringing letters from Kashi Pandits. The Kayasthas of Uttar Pradesh were declared to be Kshatriyas by a decision of the Allahabad High Court, while the Kayasthas of Bengal were declared Shudras by a decision of the Calcutta High Court.[30]

In the Konkan there is a caste which calls itself Vaishya-Vani. A Vani is a shopkeeper and like Tukaram may belong to a Kunbi-caste. The appellation Vaishya-Vani tells us that this caste claims to belong to the Vaishya *varna* (the third) in the four-rank system. A number of very low-ranking castes have started calling themselves "Valmiki". Valmiki, the mythical composer of the Ramayana was, according to popular mythology, a robber belonging to a low caste. The word Valmiki, while not laying any claim to a higher *varna*, releases the castes in future from the degradation associated with their old name.

These examples illustrate the hold which the four-rank system has on people's minds. They also give an insight into the relationship between caste and *varna*. When people show an inclination to change the caste name, they invariably try to assume names which would put them in a higher *varna*.

Government's policy at present is to give preferential treatment to people of the lower, i.e. educationally backward castes and we shall see that this has, to some extent, reversed the urge to be called Kshatriya or Brahmin, but

---

[30] *Maharashtra Dnyanakosha* (Marathi Encyclopaedia) by S. V. KETKAR, article on *Kayastha*.

the old trend is still seen to be working very powerfully.
It has been reported to the author in a personal communication, that people of the scheduled castes of Bengal have
been paying certain fees to the Registrar to get their family
names changed to Chatterji, Banerji, Mukerji, i.e. obviously
Brahmanical names.

The Marathas, politically a very conscious group, set
up for some time a strong anti-Brahmin front. On the
plateau of western Maharashtra there used to be two main
agricultural castes — the Maratha and the Kunbi — who
were separately enumerated till the census of 1911. In
the 1921 census the Kunbi caste had become so small in the
districts of western Maharashtra that a combined caption
"Maratha and Kunbi" was adopted. In 1945-46, the
author, while doing anthropometric work in this area,
found no man claiming to be Kunbi. We have seen above
that Marathas claim to be Kshatriyas and it was averred
by Maratha leaders that Kunbi and Maratha were the same
and that the appellation Kunbi should be given up. In
western Maharashtra, especially in the districts of the
Deccan plateau, this has come to pass, but though unity
has been achieved on the political front, as regards marriage, the Marathas marry as a rule only Marathas and not
those who were formerly classed as Kunbi.

We thus see that irrespective of the economic situation or influence, there are some traditional values attached to certain ranks and that it is the endeavour of the
lower ranks to reach the higher.

The four-*varṇa* system, as mentioned above, is based
on the four primary ranks called Brahmin, Kshatriya,
Vaishya and Shudra. In Maharashtra the rank called
Brahmin includes all the castes which call themselves Brahmin of one sort or another. It is thus made up of one
caste-cluster which goes under the name of Brahmin. The
rank Kshatriya is made up of Maratha, Kayastha, Khatri
and numerous other castes like "Somavamshi Vadval",
"Sahasrarjuna-vamshi Kshatriya Patwegar", "Somavamshi Pathare Kshatriya", etc.

It will be seen that some of the older castes like Maratha and Kayastha do not have the word Kshatriya as part of their caste label. The new claimants all have Kshatriya added to the better known caste names which had belonged to them before claiming the Kshatriya *varṇa*. Secondly even as regards the older ranks of Kshatriya, they were made up of more than one caste-cluster. The same is the case with the rank called Vaishya. The indigenous traders of the plateau used to call themselves Kunbi. In the coastal districts of Maharashtra there is a Marathi-speaking trading caste which calls itself Vaishya-Vani. Other trading castes are of northern origin and retain their northern names, which sometimes have words like Vaishya or Bania as part of their caste names.

The author does not know of any caste in the Shudra *Varṇa*, which uses the word "Shudra" as a part of the caste name. The word "Shudra" has been applied to certain castes for centuries. People other than the Shudras use it while speaking about them; but the castes which are so designated never use it for themselves. They will give their caste name as Kumbhar, Parit, Mahar, etc. The author feels that the '*jāti*' system which allowed innumerable different endogamous groups to live separately is entirely different from the '*varṇa*' system which divided all society into four ranks. The '*jāti*' organization or something very like it was in existence in India for a long time, the author thinks, even prior to the coming in of the Aryans. The '*varṇa*' organization belonged to the society which brought the Vedas to India. It seems native to the Aryan immigrants. In the course of time the *varṇa* system was modified and the *varṇa* and *jāti* systems were interwoven together to form a very elaborate ranking system.

References show that this was a system which had names for two ranks viz. (1) Brahma and (2) Kshatra or Rajanya. The third rank was made up of 'Vis' i.e. all the subjects. From this later on came the (3) 'Vaishya' rank. All these three ranks had common gods and common ritual. To this society a fourth rank was added. This was

(4) Shudra. From the very first this rank had no rights to Aryan ritual.

The fourth rank was made up of a vast population outside the ranks of the conquerors. This large group of people were given a name, but the conquerers did not know much about the internal structure of the fourth rank.

The second peculiarity of this rank is that it contains more caste-clusters than any of the other three ranks. Besides most of the artisan castes mentioned above it also contains caste-clusters following the profession of fishermen, boatmen, shepherds, buffalo-herders, some types of cow-herds, and pig-keepers, as also all those castes which comprise landless tenants or agricultural labourers and some types of farmers. It contains over fifty caste-clusters, each cluster containing from five to over a dozen separate endogamous castes.

In yet another way this *varṇa* is peculiar. The castes labelled "untouchable" also belonged to this *varṇa*. The theoretical equality of castes in a *varṇa* is so disturbed by this that instead of calling the untouchables a part of the fourth *varṇa* in Tamilnad a new *varṇa*, "Panchama" (fifth) was created for these.

Another phenomenon to remember about the *varṇa*-system is that while there was and still is great rivalry among the first three *varṇas* the fourth as a *varṇa* has not figured in it.

Besides the *varṇa*-system, which puts whole caste-clusters together in one rank making four ranks in all, there is in existence another ranking system, which is not written down in detail in ancient records. It was in existence and had been well described by anthropologists (GHURYE, HUTTON, etc.). Some modern anthropologists have noticed and described it in detail for some restricted areas. This ranking system applies to small areas, and is something on which many people in that area agree. There are always some dissenting voices but it is seen in operation at certain times when the people gather together for eating or have to sit together on some other occasion.

In certain studies,[31] it was seen that at the time of the annual fair at the village temple, everybody in the village is fed at a public feast. All people in the village are given certain tasks to perform on this day. Tasks which are connected with the cooking of the meal, cutting vegetables and bringing water are allotted to people of the higher castes, while tasks like sweeping the temple precincts, bringing fire-wood for cooking, cleaning after meals, are performed by the lower castes. Meals are served by the higher castes to the lower castes. This ranking is found for castes within each *varṇa* in such a way that while a great number of castes are ranked as belonging to the *varṇa,* some may be denied the status of belonging to it. A caste may lay claim to a certain social status and call itself by a new name, but while the new name may be accepted by the people around, the status claimed may not be accepted. For example a caste called Daivadnya Sonar in Maharashtra, belonging to the caste-cluster Sonar (gold-smith), has claimed to belong to the Brahmin *varṇa* by claiming to be Brahmins. This claim has not been accepted by the Brahmin castes. How this claim has affected the standing of this caste among (a) the Sonar caste-cluster, (b) among artisan caste clusters and (c) among Shudras to which the Sonar caste-cluster is reckoned, has not been studied. We shall take up these questions a little later.

---

[31] *"Intergroup relations in rural communities".* I. KARVE and Y. B. DAMLE. Shortly to be published by the Deccan College, Poona.

CHAPTER II

CASTE—A HISTORICAL SURVEY

The description I have given of the caste system does not differ from that given by other anthropologists, but the significance of the various aspects of the system described is different because of what I think is the nature and function of this system.

I have already noted that the Hindu society made up of castes was envisaged by older anthropologists as a society which split into castes according to the occupations taken up by people. It was said that the caste system with its ranking device of the four *varṇas* was a creation of the Brahmins to ensure race purity, or rather the purity of the colour (*varṇa*) of their skin. The caste system was found to have analogies to certain other social systems of the world. It was asserted by Professor GHURYE that in fundamentals it did not differ from the class system of the modern Western societies. It was also stated that there was a time when the numerous castes were not existent, that taboos on inter-caste marriage were not strict and that continuous splitting of larger groups has led to the presence of the enormous number of mutually exclusive castes.

It is this theoretical framework which I feel does not tally with my field experience nor with ancient records and it is these points and my interpretation of caste as a phenomenon in the total cultural picture that I propose to discuss now.

The word for caste used throughout Sanskrit literature and in Pali, and Jain Prakrit literature was *jāti*. Sometimes, very rarely, the word *yoni* was used and at some places the word *kula*. The word *jāti* is not found in the oldest literature.[1] The word found there is *varṇa*. The Vedas mention sometimes two *varṇas*, sometimes three *varṇas*. In later hymns a fourth *varṇa* was added. This is the beginning of the four-*varṇa* system.

Varṇa in later classical Sanskrit generally means a colour and so it has been argued that the four-*varṇa* system was based on the distinction of skin colour between the Aryans and the pre-Aryan residents of India. *Varṇa* undoubtedly means colour in later literature, but it is not used in that sense in the Vedas at all. The word *varṇa* means in early sacred literature and in grammatical works a *class*. This is very clear in treatises on grammar. The various consonants are arranged according to the place of origin in the throat and mouth and called *kaṇṭhya*, *oṣṭhya* (guttural, labial), etc. Also the alphabet in a given order is called the *varṇa-mala* a garland of *varṇas*. The *varṇa* thus suggests not only a class, but an order of precedence. The word *varṇa*, when used for describing human society also means class in a particular order.

---

[1] See footnote 10, p. 53.

Below is given the translation of a passage from *Chhāndogya Upanishad* (ca. 400 to 500 B.C.) which is interesting because the doctrine is similar to one developed much later. Only, the word used here is *yoni* :

Those who behave in a pleasing way and eat pleasant things get into a pleasing *yoni* like Brahmani-*yoni* or Vaishya-*yoni* or Kshatriya-*yoni*. Those however who behave (or work) in a filthy (evil smelling) manner and eat such things get into a filthy *yoni* like horse-*yoni* or pig-*yoni* or Chandala-*yoni*.

This passage enunciates the doctrine of rebirth and the dependence of the type of birth on the type of actions and food. (Cf. Bhagavadgītā — 7.21, 22, 23; 17.3, 8, 9, 10).

It is obvious that Brahmin, Kshatriya and Vaishya on the one hand and horse, pig and *chandala* on the other are comparable categories according to the author of this passage. *Chandala* is the name of a low caste, the members of which were supposed to be untouchables. '*Yoni*' has thus the sense of biological as well as sociological classes. We find that '*jāti*' and '*kula*' have also been used in the same sense. In this passage instead of using the more generic *varṇa*-term, Shudra as opposed to Brahman, Kshatriya and Vaishya, the lowest of many *jātis*, namely *chandala* is mentioned.

Foisting a later meaning of the word in contexts where that meaning was not known, creates a wrong idea. This type of reasoning based on new interpretations of old words is found in other places too in classical literature.[2]

The word *varna* is used in two different ways in the Vedic literature. Sometimes two *varnas* are mentioned as Arya-*varna* and Dasa-*varna*, the Arya class and the Dasa class. In this expression the new immigrant Aryas are contrasted to the old population, Dasa.[3] More often the two *varnas* mentioned are Brahma (Brahmins) and *Rajanya* or *Kshatra* (Kshatriyas). Both these were within the Arya society and so the reference cannot possibly be to the skin colour. Whenever the three *varnas* of the Aryan society were mentioned, the third was called *vish*.[4] The meaning of the word "*vish*" is "all", "the multitude". They were the commoners over whom the king ruled. This becomes clear in the expression for king, *visham-pati*, which means the master (*pati*) of the *vish* (the word is used in the plural to suggest the human multitude.)

In a sense then there were only two *varnas*, which were lifted out of the multitude, which had special designations and they were the Brahmin, the magician-priests —

---

[2] The words *rajan* and *kshatriya* . . . . . .

[3] The word *Dasa* from later Vedic period came to mean "a slave". The historical analogy here is to the word "Slav" for eastern Europeans.

[4] The above words were those used in the Vedas. The word for the Brahmin caste creates a good deal of confusion in the minds of readers not acquainted with Sanskrit literature and pronunciation. There is a *varna* called Brahma or Brahmana; there is a group of sacred books also called Brahmana (neuter gender); and there is a personified god, the creator, called Brahman (masculine gender). In order to avoid confusion as far as possible I have adopted the following scheme: The *varna* and the caste-cluster is spelled with the English spelling Brahmin; the sacred books are written Brahmana ('s); the Ultimate Truth is written as Brahman (neuter gender, of which the nominative singular is Brahma); the god is written as Brahma, (which is the nominative singular of Brahman masculine gender).

(the great ones) — and the Rajanya, the nobles and kings — (the shining ones).

It is wrong to suppose that the *varṇa* system arose out of a consciousness of racial distinctions as indicated by skin colour.[5] The Aryan world was made up of the three classes of priests, nobles and commoners. All the people worshipped the same gods and underwent the same rituals from birth to death. One such ritual was the initiation ceremony, called the investiture with the sacred thread,[6] which involved a magical performance imitating birth.[7]

The Aryans came into contact with the conquered non-Aryan masses, and made a place for them which was the lowest *varṇa*. This was called Shudra.[8] In a late hymn the Shudras are envisaged as having arisen from the feet of the First Being and so assigned to menial work. The Shudras had no right to the Aryan ritual, could never perform the rites to become *dwija*.[9]

This in short is the *varṇa* system of the Aryas. The *jātis* are described for the first time in a compilation called Manusmṛti,[10] which is ascribed to the mythical first

---

[5] The word *varṇa* may be derived from *vṛ*, to choose. *Varṇa* are the chosen ones, while everybody else is *vish*, i.e. the multitude. Out of these, the two, the Brahmin and the Rajanya have special designations, they are lifted out as the 'chosen' ones. According to Dr. S. M. KATRE, it may also be traced to the root *vṛ* = to cover, which semantically indicates an act of separation and consequently of choosing or selecting.

[6] The Parsees, who follow the old Iranian religion, akin to the Aryan religion, also have such a ceremony, for both men and women.

[7] Everyone who underwent this ceremony was called *dwija*, the twice-born. In later times this ceremony came to be performed predominantly by Brahmins only and so they alone came to be called *dwija*.

[8] The meaning of the word and its etymology are not certain. Perhaps like *dasa*, it was a tribal name, which came to stand for the lowest rank.

[9] In the attempts of the castes to rise higher, the claim to perform the thread ceremony came first.

[10] The Indian literary tradition is as follows :—The oldest texts are called in English the Vedic literature. This consists of (1) the four Vedas and (2) the Brahmanas with their Upanishads. The

king Manu. In this book Manu describes the origin and the rise of *jātis* in the following manner.

He starts with four *varṇas* as something given or primary and derives all castes as being due to mixtures of these pure *varṇas*. Let us take the letters B b, K k, V v, and S s to stand for Brahmin, Kshatriya, Vaishya and Shudra males and females respectively. When a Brahmin man marries a woman from any of the three other *varṇas*,

four Vedas are books of hymns containing prayers and supplications, magic incantations and a few verses of philosophical import. The Ṛgveda is supposed to be the oldest. The Samaveda which is a book of songs comes next. Yajurveda which in its older form is made up of instructions in prose about sacrifices and hymns is supposed to be next and Atharvaveda, a book of magic incantations and philosophical doctrines, is supposed to be be the last. The four books contain a lot of material which is common and considered anthropologically they appear to belong together. The Atharvaveda which contains very old magic and medicine has certain verses which Prof. Lüders compared, in his lectures given in the University of Berlin and attended by the author, to old Germanic magical incantations. The four books seem to contain the old Aryan cultural capital of religion, song, magic and medicine. This apparently was all mixed together. Indian tradition says that a wise sage took in hand this material and brought order into it and made it into the four Vedas as above.

The Brahmanas are prose books, mainly manuals to be used at the time of different sacrifices. They contain myths, parables, philological speculations and also books within books called Upanishads. These latter are purely philosophical speculations about god and the ultimate reality, rebirth, etc.

This literature traditionally is purely orthodox (Sanatana) literature though one finds in it definite beginnings of later schisms and dissensions leading to Buddhism and Jainism.

After Upanishads the literature is vast and varied. Some of it is religious, some in the form of folk-tales, some epical, poetry and drama and a great number of commentaries on religious literature. Although the three doctrines, viz. the Orthodox, the Buddhist and the Jain have separate literary and philosophical traditions, each borrows heavily from and gives much to the other two.

The religious tradition of the orthodoxy is called variously Sanatana, Vaidic, Brahmanic and lastly Hindu. Its 'Śruti' means that which is 'heard'. This is the revealed literature consisting there will be three castes (Bk, Bv and Bs) ; a Kshatriya marrying a woman of the two lower *varṇas* will give two new castes (Kv and Ks) and similarly a Vaishya marrying a Shudra woman will give one more caste (Vs). Thus six castes emerge by a man of a higher *varṇa* marrying a woman of a lower *varṇa*. Similarly if a man of a lower *varṇa* marries a woman of a higher *varṇa*, we shall have six more castes (Kb, Vb, Vk, Sb, Sk and Sv). The first type of marriage, though not favoured as the best practice, was however allowed as not being too bad, and was called *anuloma*[11] marriage, i.e., marriage of a man of a higher

of the Vedas and Brahmanas and Upanishads. 'Smṛti' is that which is 'remembered' and consists of over a dozen books the first supposed to be composed by 'Manu' the first king and later by various sages. The Smṛti books are called in English "law-books" and Manu's Smṛti is called "the code of Manu". This has created confusion. At no time was any Smṛti given the sanction of any political authority. There were in existence always more than one Smṛti. Any point before the ancient judges could be disputed according to different Smṛtis. Smṛtis differed in many vital points. Smṛtis enunciated principles of behaviour which went against ancient practices. One Smṛti disputed what another had said and lastly among rules of behaviour there was always a chapter called "Kali-varjya-Prakaraṇam" which told of practices not allowed in this present Kali-age. This disposed of practices like beef-eating, begetting children on one's wife from a stranger or from a brother of the husband. These were mentioned as behaviours of ancient kings and sages but were no longer respectable. Smṛtis were never 'law'. They were a record of 'good practices'.

This did not exhaust authorities considered as norms of some kind. 'Vṛddhāchāra' means "the behaviour of the elders". This principle is not written down at all and consists of the behaviour of those considered as elders and leaders in a society. This has been a 'common sense' principle found in many didactic poems and also in Bhagavadgitā. Shri Krishna says in Bhagavadgitā (Bhag. 3rd canto, verses 22, 23 and 24). "I have nothing which has got to be done. I have nothing which I have not obtained. Still, I go on behaving as others as if I had goals to attain. People who follow my example everywhere would come to perish if I did not keep active as I am doing now."

[11] "In the direction of hair-growth". If one strokes an animal in such a direction it is tolerated but if one does it in the other direction, the hair is rumpled. The animal gets angry.

status to a woman of a lower status. This is what is called hypergamy. The second type of mating was called
pratiloma[12] and was frowned upon. The status of the first
six hybrid castes was higher than the second group of six
castes. These twelve represented the first crosses.

From the four *varṇas* by just two crossings one gets a
total of 204 castes as follows :

(1)	*Anuloma* and *pratiloma* castes after first crossing	12
(2)	Crossing of six *anuloma* castes among themselves	15
(3)	The same with man and woman in the reverse order	15
(4)	Crossing of the original four *varṇas* with six *anuloma* and six *pratiloma* castes	48
(5)	Crossing of six *pratiloma* castes among themselves and with the four *varṇas*, i.e. same as (2), (3), (4)	78
(6)	Inter-crossing between the six *anuloma* and six *pratiloma* castes	36
	Total	204

Manu gives names of some castes and their status too, depending upon who the father and the mother of the person were. He however was not able to name each of the
above crosses.[13] It is known that new castes have arisen
out of a mixture of two castes and holding an intermediate
position, but the number of such castes is very small and
this explanation of Manu does not seem to be based on in-
quiry and observation but rather on the position of bastards
in the courts of the kings and a flare for mathematical
speculation, for which Indians were well-known in ancient
times.

This account makes it probable that the Aryans did
not have *jāti*, but still there might have been castes in
India. The guess is strengthened by the treatment of caste
by Manu. The Vedic literature consists of hymns, ritual,

---

[12] Against the direction in which the hair grows.
[13] *Manu-Smṛti*, Canto 10, in the original or "Laws of Manu" by
G. BUHLER. pp. 401-430, Clarendon Press, Oxford, 1886.

sacrificial procedures and philosophical speculations. The references to *varṇa* are also very few. But Manu's book is a manual dealing with the daily life of the people, the rights and duties of different groups, instructions to a king about how to rule, etc. Here Manu has to take account of *jāti*, but he wants to bring this phenomenon into the sphere of the structure known to him and which is reported in books which are sacred to him, viz. *varṇa*. He therefore gives a very artificial etiology to explain the existence of castes. He did not say that castes arose out of occupational specialization; he resorted to the mathematical device of permutation and combination to derive all the castes. A man brought up in the traditions of the Aryans attempted to account for a type of grouping not understood by him and tried to interpret the phenomenon in the light of his experience.

It is probable that something very like castes were in India even before the Aryans came and the Aryans as a conquering people placed their three *varṇas* at the head of the whole indigenous society. In this process a number of indigenous elements were incorporated into the known *varṇas*. Brahmins were recruiting their ranks; the Kshatriyas gladly contracted marriages with princesses of reigning non-Aryan houses; and the Vish, from their original position as the toiling masses, were themselves emerging as a wealthy class owning slaves. Bhagavadgita, which is a part of the epic Mahabharata, still enumerated the duties of different *varṇas* in old terms. Learning was the duty of the Brahmins; ruling and fighting bravely that of the Kshatriyas; tending of cattle, farming the land and engaging in trade was the work of the Vaishya (Vedic Vish) and serving all these three that of the Shudras.

In the early Buddhist literature the Vaishya emerges as the wealthy merchant. The cowherd and the farmer are looked down upon. This transformation of the Aryan Vish from a toiling commoner to a wealthy merchant class shows the new adjustment to a new social situation presented by a mass of conquered people readily available for all hard and menial work.

In India each caste at present has a separate living area. This was the case in ancient India also if one takes into account the oldest records which describe cities and villages. These are the story literature in Prakrit of the Buddhists and the Jains.[14] This literature presents a picture of how people, commoners, merchants, kings and priests lived in ancient India. The picture is that of a full-fledged caste-society with different parts of the cities allotted to different castes.

Archaeologists hold that the semi-nomadic pastoral Vedic Aryans destroyed the Indus civilization and possibly also the city of Harappa.[15] In the excavations of Harappa a whole street was found with stone mortars, where cereals, perhaps rice, were either husked or pounded into flour. The western archaeologists have called it the slave quarters, or places of government enterprise where slaves pounded cereals.[16] That scores of "mortars" were found in one "street" is a fact. The rest is conjecture. I venture to give an alternative conjecture. Probably it was a street lived in by a caste-like group, who specialized in pounding rice.

Be this as it may, looking at the Sanskrit record itself we have no evidence that caste was "created" by race-conscious Brahmins. It appears as if the Aryans came upon the phenomenon of caste and fitted it into a scheme known to them. The union of *varṇa* and *jāti* is a matter of fusion of two systems from two cultures.

If *jātis* had existed since pre-Aryan times and if they were not an Aryan invention, how could they have been formed? We have absolutely no ancient records to guide us, but certain analogies of this institution with others may give a clue. Also the processes of caste-making were going on throughout history and are happening even at present. A study of these may possibly give us an insight into the process.

---

[14] See passages quoted in the appendix.

[15] Stuart PIGGOT — *Pre-historic India.* Chap. VI & VII, in the Pelican Book series — 1950.

[16] *Ibid.,* p. 154.

Endogamy, a region of spread and an internal agency for social control are features in which a caste has similarity with a tribe. The tribal area of a tribe is generally exclusive to a tribe. There are, however, examples of multi-tribal tracts and multi-tribal villages in certain areas of Africa. I have pointed out in a study[17] how each village has its habitation area divided sometimes sharply and sometimes roughly into areas of different castes. Again within a caste-area there are divisions according to lineages and clans. Thus a caste is, in its most important features, a tribe-like group. Even the hierarchy, which is found among castes is found in certain multi-tribal areas. In Africa, the Ruanda-Urundi area is shared by three tribes. The Watutsi are the rulers and conquerors, the Bahutu are workers on land, are the conquered people and represent the serfs, while the Batwas are pigmies and live in the nearby forests and hold a position between the two other tribes.

We have also multi-tribal tracts in Rhodesia and East Africa where each tribe seems to specialize in one or more crafts. On market days, people from each tribe bring goods for which they are known. Some bring bark-cloth, some woven cotton-cloth, some pottery, and some are specialists in wooden vessels. As regards agricultural produce, there seems to be some little specialization too. Similar markets are held in the multi-caste and multi-tribal forest areas of Andhra and Orissa in India and each caste and each tribe brings the things for which they are known. The mode of tribal intercourse is also peripheral and tangential as in the case of castes. Like castes again the tribes occupying the same region may or may not be of the same racial origin. In the case of the Ruanda-Urundi area, the three-tribe society is made up of three races; in other parts of Africa tribes belonging to the same race live separately in the same area. This is especially the case in the very populated regions of Rhodesia. In the forested regions of India we have similar cases too. In the Nilgiris

[17] The structure of an Indian Village, *Deccan College Bulletin*, 1958.

the Toda, the Badaga and the Kota live as separate tribes with specialized occupations. The Toda are racially different from the Kota and the Badaga. The latter two seem to be racially similar. In Orissa Gond, Koya, Bhatra, Saora and Porja come to the same markets. Each is a separate endogamous tribe, not a separate race.

Castes over a wide area may not show much racial difference, whatever the status of the different castes. On the other hand castes living side by side, following identical professions and bearing the same name as applied to a caste-cluster, may show great physical differences. That castes following the same profession and living in the same large linguistic region may belong to different racial stocks, was recognized by anthropologists. But on the other hand, it was also said by Sir Herbert RISLEY that within an area like e.g. the Punjab, all castes were physically nearer to each other than to any other caste in the neighbouring region. This argument implies that castes arose in a homogeneous population through fission following occupational specialization. Then again, while Dr. GHURYE concedes this for the Punjab, he does not think that it is true for other regions where, according to him, caste formation and ranking was due to an effort of the Brahmins to maintain racial purity. In the quotation given previously he uses a very curious word with reference to Brahmins. He calls them "prospectors".[18] What the Brahmins were prospecting for one does not know. In any case we have here two separate or simultaneous etiologies of caste, one based on fission and the other on a desire for racial purity. It has been shown in recent work that castes occupying the same rank in the same region are not necessarily similar in physical appearance and measurements, nor do castes occupying different levels in the social status show necessarily physical differences.[19]

It is here that the analogy of a multi-tribal society becomes fruitful. Different units live separately in endo-

[18] Was it the influence of the school of ELLIOT & PERRY ?
[19] KARVE and DANDEKAR, loc. cit.

gamous, semi-autonomous cells in such societies. Such units are tribes, or rather, parts of great tribes. Each part in its wandering separates from the great tribe and finds itself accommodating to new neighbours. There is no political pressure to amalgamate. Such tribal units might mingle to form newer, larger units or may remain separate.

The argument about the tribe-like separateness of castes does not rest on racial separateness. Tribes in an area can belong to the same racial stock and yet keep themselves separate. In Africa, Australia, America, Asia, in the primitive regions of India, there are separate tribes which belong to the same racial stock, but which occupy the same region and speak the same language or, sometimes, languages belonging to the same family. In historical times we have examples of the Germanic tribes called the Goths, the Saxons, the Angles, etc. Anthropologists do not talk in terms of fission or segmentation of a single unit when mentioning the present tribal populations or the tribe or peoples referred to in history. There are examples of a few castes which have been formed by fission, but castes in general are not so formed and are as independent and separate as tribes are. This separateness is sometimes seen in deep-going differences in the patterns of social behaviour, sometimes in cultural-historical traditions and sometimes in physical differences. There is no one instrument of analysis fine enough or comprehensive enough to demonstrate the separateness in all cases.

An illustration would make my meaning clear. A linguistic region with its many castes is not comparable to one picture cut into different pieces as in a jig-saw puzzle. A caste-cluster made up of various castes following similar professions (e.g. Kumbhar = potters, Sonar = goldsmiths, etc.) and known by one term is also not a jig-saw puzzle. The region with its many castes, as also a caste-cluster with its many castes, are more like a patchwork quilt where even the patches, which have similar colour and shape, may have different origins. The red patches may look similar, but one may be a piece of a bedspread, another of an old curtain, a third from a shirt, a fourth from a blouse, and so on. Also all the pieces making together one quilt at a particular time may have been incorporated into the quilt at different times. Just as the original sources of the pieces are different, so also the time of their incorporation may be different.

In order to make this analogy applicable to the Hindu society it will be necessary to show that castes within a caste-cluster are of different origins and that a number of them have come into a region at different times. It will also be necessary to demonstrate the original entity out of which a piece in the patchwork has come, that the bedspread, the shirt, etc., existed at one time and that pieces of it can be traced elsewhere. This demonstration for all castes of a region is impossible; for even a few castes it is, if not impossible, extremely difficult. A long programme of systematic work may solve some problems, but those that require historical research are indeed really difficult in a land and in a society which has been well known for its lack of historical records. I give below a few examples known to me. Some are well established, some are conjectures based on epigraphical and literary records.

Some time about the 7th or 8th century a tribe or a group of tribes from Central Asia came into India. They succeeded in founding an empire called by the present day historians the Empire of the Gurjara Pratihara. Gurjara was apparently the Sanskritised name of the tribe. Pratihara was possibly the name (also Sanskritised) of some clans or families. It is not clear what it meant. The Gurjara empire vanished about the 12th century. The empire extended from Kanoj (in western U.P.) to Punjab and southwards towards Gujarat. There are three areas, which are supposed to have been called after the tribe. There are two districts in the Punjab called Gujaranwala and Gujarat and one province (now the separate state) called Gujarat, to the north of Maharashtra. Endogamous groups calling themselves Gujar are spread today from the Punjab to Maharashtra. In the sub-Himalayan region there are Muslim Gujars, who herd buffaloes. In the

Delhi region, there are Gujars who till land, there is also another caste called Gujar, which has lived as a poor nomadic people since the days of Emperor Akbar. In northern Maharashtra there are farmers who call themselves Gujars and among whom the author found a clan name Padhyar, obviously derived from Pratihara. Among Rajputs there is a Gujar clan and there is in Maharashtra a Jain caste called Gujar, who are traders. Among the Marathas too there is a Gujar clan.

One cannot be sure that all those who call themselves Gujar are derived from the Gurjara tribe, but a number may be so derived, when one takes into consideration the extent of the medieval empire and the regions in which the Gujar castes are found. A tribe dispersed over a large area in four linguistic regions. In most regions it kept itself as a separate entity, took up different occupations and fitted itself into the caste hierarchy on different rungs. This process can be roughly illustrated as follows :

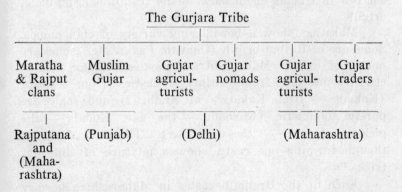

The Gurjara Tribe

Maratha & Rajput clans	Muslim Gujar	Gujar agriculturists	Gujar nomads	Gujar agriculturists	Gujar traders
Rajputana and (Maharashtra)	(Punjab)	(Delhi)		(Maharashtra)	

None of these castes know of the Gurjara Pratihara empire or are aware of the existence of the other castes. The nomads are low down in the caste ranking. The agriculturists are much higher, but according to the *varṇa* scheme of ranking, they are Shudras. The traders rank higher and would be in the Vaishya *varṇa*. Those Gujars who have merged into the Rajputs may be said to have reached the Kshatriya ranking.

The Gurjars have thus entered into the caste society of four different linguistic regions in different ways and at different levels.[20]

While we have here an example of a tribe spreading over wide areas and taking up different positions in each area and remaining as a separate entity, there are also examples of mingling. The probable absorption of a part of the Gurjara tribe into Rajput and Maratha castes has been referred to above. If one takes into account the clan names among Rajputs and Marathas this becomes quite evident. The name Chauhan, written in earlier records as Chahumana is probably of Central Asiatic origin — perhaps belonging to the Huns. A Hun king Toramana once ruled in Northern India. Another name, Paramara also seems to be of Central Asiatic origin. According to Rajput traditions, while other clans trace their origin from the sun and the moon, these two clans are supposed to have arisen out of fire. Even Brahmins apparently could not succeed in tracing them back to the traditional sun-moon origins.

Marathas show a bewildering variety of clan names. Some are of Rajput origin (Chavan, Pavar, etc.) some are names of extinct Maharashtra dynasties (Kadam, Sinde, etc.), some are from extinct dynasties from Andhra (Kakade — from Kakatiya of Andhra?) and some are purely totemistic (Kurhade — the axe, Kudale — the pick-axe, Landge — the wolf, etc.). Thus the Marathas though forming one caste, show a mixture of different tribes.[21]

Each of the Brahmin castes in Maharashtra is very probably of a different origin and this has already been indicated above. It was also shown how the period of their habitation in Maharashtra might be different. A similar case was made out for the difference in origins of the vari-

---

[20] Some castes which have the word *Gujar* as a part of their name may not be derived from the "Gujar" tribes at all, but may have taken up the word for the sake of social prestige.

[21] Racially however they seem to be similar.

ous Kumbhar castes. It was indicated that some of the agricultural castes were of tribal origin.

The process of caste-making has not stopped. New castes are coming into being even in the present age, as the following example will show.

This is from a tribe called Savara (Sanskrit Shabara) in Orissa and Andhra. This tribe is spread from the northern Andhra districts of Vishakhapatnam and Srikakulam to northern Orissa (north of Cuttack). In each jungle area they are an endogamous group. Marriages are not known outside of the immediate neighbourhood, which may extend to a hundred square miles. The Savara area is cut up by rivers, jungles and mountains. The people in the south do not know of the existence of the people in the north. The southern Savara are a primitive tribe, who live independently of the others in their jungle villages. They come occasionally to the jungle markets where they meet other jungle tribes and agricultural peoples and exchange of goods takes place. In Orissa, round about Lake Chilka I found that the Savaras came regularly to the weekly market held in a coastal village and sold firewood. The village communities were dependent on the Savara for firewood and the Savaras bought some food, cloth and pots in the market. Still they kept to their jungles. Further northwards I found that the city of Cuttack was also dependent on Savaras for firewood. The Savaras were settled in the villages round Cuttack, had become a village folk and a specialized caste and either went into the jungles to cut wood or bought it from other jungle tribes.

The process by which tribes spread over very large areas and lose contact with the parent body is found all over the world. Such a process populated all the continents of the world long before the neolithic age. Such a process has been well studied in the spread of the northern Germanic tribes in the early Christian centuries and with reference to the Bantu-speaking tribes of Africa. In Europe, tribes and parts of tribes, as they spread, amalgamated with others to form larger units. In Africa on the

H.S.—5

other hand many tribes have retained their identity and
separateness, so that one finds a number of tribes in a relatively small area.   These are the many multi-tribal areas
in Africa.   India is counted among the ancient civilized
nations and yet it also retained this separateness of spreading and wandering units as they settled into each area.
These are the castes.

There are over two thousand castes in India at present.   There are about two hundred castes in each linguistic region of India.   My contention that a caste in each
linguistic region is separate from the other castes and was
so for centuries, does not mean that there were two
thousand separate entities to start with.   There were in
India tribal groups, as also different races.   They spread
over the sub-continent, but instead of amalgamating with
others to make bigger groups, each retained its separateness.   The names of many of these groups are recorded in
India's literature.   The names of a few only need be mentioned here.   They are, Arya, Kushan, Shaka, Gurjara,
Naga, Dasa, Shabara, Malla and a hundred others.   Some
came as immigrants, others are mentioned as living in
India when the immigrants arrived.   One hears names of
different tribal groups in the protohistory of modern
Europe also, but they wandered and merged with other
folks and tribes.   In India tribes and peoples could merge
with others if they wanted. They could also live separately
for an indefinite period if they so wished.

In the two diagrams 1 and 2 the idea of how a caste
society is made is illustrated by the analogy of the patchwork quilt.   Only a few castes have been shown in the
diagram.

In diagram 1 : I, II, III, IV are Brahmin castes, each
in a slightly separate area, each with different physical
measurements and each probably inhabiting Maharashtra
for different lengths of time, varying from 2000 years to
perhaps 600 years.   The centre piece is the great Maratha
caste, which is made up of elements from central Asiatic
tribes, Rajput clans, ruling dynasties of 2000 to 1000 years
ago, elements from Dravidian-speaking peoples of Andhra

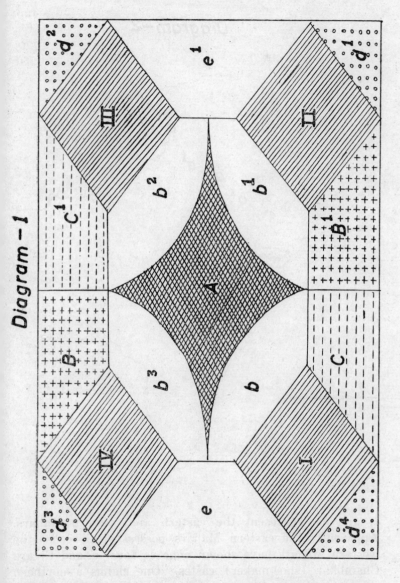

and Karnatak and lastly perhaps some primitive tribes. d, d¹, d², d³ are Kumbhar (potter) castes, each of different origin: one from Gujarat, another from the Gangetic plain, a third from Andhra, a fourth apparently of local origin.

Diagram-2

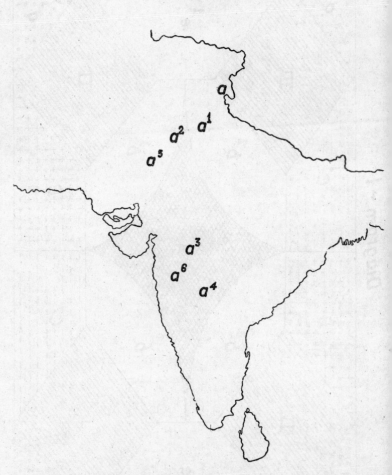

B and B¹ represent the eastern and western Mahars. Apparently the eastern Mahars possess sickle cells, the western Mahars have shown none so far. C and C¹ are Chambhar (shoe-maker) castes. One claims a northern origin and has northern customs, the second is from Karnatak. e and e¹ are Sonar (goldsmith) castes. One claims a Gujarat (Lata) origin. The other has been in residence in Maharashtra for a long time, claims to be astrologers and Brahmins. Similarly, all the other castes in the region could be represented in the diagram, although I have not done that here in order not to make it too complicated.

Diagram 2 shows the location of some of the castes which call themselves Gujar represented as a, a¹, a² etc.

I have given so many references from old literature and suggested an alternative explanation of something found in Harappa to indicate some of the reasons for my second proposition, which is that groups living apart and organized into a caste-like structure seem to have existed for a very long time in India, were there before the Aryans came and persisted up to the present. At the very beginning I pointed out that living in spatial contiguity but in comparative social separateness is a trait of tribal societies. But no tribal society in the world has as many cells within it as the Indian society.

APPENDIX TO CHAPTER II

The extracts given below are from the literature other than the Smṛtis. Long before the 10th century caste was a well described phenomenon in Hindu society. I have quoted some references *in extenso* because they show that the mental processes revealed are those of a society in which castes with their taboo on exogamy, with hierarchy and with ideas of pollution were firmly rooted.

My first reference is from a book called *Vasudeva Hindi* (the wanderings of Vasudeva). This is supposed to have been composed some time during the sixth or seventh century A.D. Vasudeva is a prince of Kshatriya origin. During the course of his wanderings he married a girl of a Vaishya caste. One day while his bride had gone to worship at a temple, he amused himself by looking on and listening to dances and singing by young boys and girls of the city. When the dancing and singing troupe saw him, they sang a song which ran as follows : "There is a big forest. The merchants are afraid to go through it because a huge fierce lion lives there. Some merchants who were compelled to cross it in order to reach a large city decided that they would keep a constant watch with drawn swords while going through the forest. As they went through the forest, they suddenly saw the big lion coming towards them on the forest path. They all stopped, ready to defend themselves. As the lion came slowly along the path a pretty female fox came to him and he mated with her. When the merchants saw this, they all laughed and feared no longer. They said, "That cannot be a lion when he mates with a fox." Vasudeva heard the song and knew that it was aimed at him and so he went into the street and scolded the troupe.

This particular union was between a Kshatriya man (Vasudeva) and a girl of the Vaishya caste, i.e., one immediately below him in the *varṇa* status. This type of marriage was allowed by Manu and ancient usage, but the story shows that the popular attitude reflects the caste sentiments of today. Marriage outside the caste was not tolerated. In another story the same Vasudeva is shown to have mated with a girl who was supposed to belong to an untouchable caste. It turned out later that she was really not an untouchable but somebody else. These stories are of special interest to students of society. Vasudeva obviously is a popular hero. He journeyed far and wide. Each change of place involved him in an adventure with fabulous birds and beasts or demons or thieves. He comes out successful always with a marriage or two at the end. Physically he does things not possible for an ordinary man. On the mental level, he is a very clever man, solves riddles that baffle other men, plays dice better than others, plays and understands music as nobody can. On the social level also he does things that others cannot do. As a prince it is his privilege to marry any commoner. That is what he does when he marries Bandhumati, the daughter of a merchant. He is made slightly ridiculous. The society cannot however stand his mating with an untouchable girl. He does it and ultimately that girl turns out not to be an untouchable at all.

The other examples are from a story book called Panchtantra.[22] In one story, a man (*Gorambho Rajasevakas*) who is called a cleaner (*Grihasammarjanakas*) and who apparently cleaned the king's palace, was driven out from a house because he occupied a place reserved for Brahmins. A verse says: "A mean man is turned against you by the slightest ill-turn, just as the Brahmins are polluted by the slightest thing." The same book also shows that as soon as a man becomes a Sanyasin, he is outside the pale of the caste society and could accept food and shelter from anybody.

The same book has two stories, which show that caste sentiments were the same as those after 1000 A.D. The

[22] KIELHORN'S edition, p. 22, line 5.

first is a well known story but needs to be told in this context. "There was a potter. Once when he was drunk, he
fell down on potsherds, hitting his forehead against a
sharp broken piece. His forehead had a big gash, which
took a long time to heal (owing to his bad diet). It left
a deep red scar. There came a great famine and this
potter together with other people went to another kingdom.
The king saw this hefty man and thought, here indeed was
a great warrior who faced his enemies squarely, as the big
gash on his forehead showed. The king gave him much
money and employed him in a very high rank in his army.
Once the kingdom was invaded by an enemy and warriors
were going out to give battle. At that time the king asked
the potter as to how he happened to get the gash in the
forehead. The potter told the truth. The king was both
enraged and ashamed at his folly, and wanted to drive
away the potter. The potter begged the king to give him
a chance to show the king his prowess in war. The king
declined and told the following story : 'A lion while hunting once came upon a fox cub, but it was so small that he
pitied it and brought it to his wife, who had two cubs of
her own. The three cubs were nursed by the lioness and
grew up together. One day, while playing together, they
saw an elephant pass. The lion cubs, seeing the hereditary enemy, roared and lashed their tails and were going to
attack. The fox was afraid, dissuaded the lion cubs from
doing such a foolhardy thing and ran home, followed by
the other two cubs. They all told this incident to their
mother, who got the fox cub aside, told him who he really
was, and said, "Son, you are brave, you have learned all
there is to learn; you are also handsome, but in your line
big game is not killed. Go away before my sons realize
who you are." ' After telling this story, the king drove
away the potter.

The third series of references is found in a Sanskrit
drama called *Mudra-Rakshasa*. It tells the story of how
Chanakya, a Brahmin, killed all the men of the reigning
house of Nanda, put Chandragupta Maurya on the throne
and succeeded in getting Rakshasa, the minister of the

Nandas to become the chief minister of Chandragupta. The play is supposed to have been written during or before the fifth century A.D. Some think that it was written a few centuries before Christ.

In the very first act, a man is mentioned as Kayastha and his profession is that of a professional writer. His writing is supposed to be beautiful and legible as against that of Brahmins versed in Shrauta-Karma. Terms of contempt are used for him saying "A Kayastha after all is of no consequence." Here a caste is mentioned, which has been well known in India as a caste of writers. People of this caste were always employed by kings and courtiers, were valued as loyal servants and have always held a position lower than that of the Kshatriyas. This passage also mentions another fact about the caste. A Brahmin was learned, as he knew by heart a dozen texts. He could read and also knew all the rules of grammar, but his writing was always primitive. There is a saying in Sanskrit *yā vidyā sā kanṭhagatā* meaning, knowledge is that which is on your tongue. Right into the Peshwa times, i.e. into the 19th century, Brahmins lived up to this ideal. The Councillor of the Peshwas was a very holy Brahmin known for his learning and piety. I had recently the opportunity to see his handwriting and it was like that of a first-form child, which has just learned to write. The importance of this reference is that we have here a caste which has a name which does not mean anything in Sanskrit. The meaning of the word "kayastha" is obscure. The occupation of the group as writers is however well known. We have thus a true caste. The difficulty as regards many other castes is that the caste name reveals the occupation and one cannot conclusively prove that the reference is to a "caste" and not just to an occupational group. However, I feel that all such references are to occupational castes.

In the same drama in the seventh act, Rakshasa begs Chanakya not to embrace him, because he had been polluted by the touch of two Chandals (the executioners). Further, in the same drama, one notices again and again, that men of high caste sat on a higher seat, while those of the lower castes sat on the bare ground.

The third set of references are from *Dhammapada Attha Katha* supposed to have been written by Buddhaghoṣa about 400 A.D. The stories themselves seem to be of a much older origin. One purports to be the story of what actually happened to the clan of the Buddha. It is thus à narrative of events which happened in the seventh century B.C. The other stories reflect the usage of Buddhaghoṣa's time, and, we can also assume, of a few centuries earlier.

The name of the king who ruled the kingdom of Kosala in the days of Buddha was Pasenadi. Buddha used to live many times near the capital city and was often visited by king Pasenadi. The king however had the feeling that neither Buddha nor his followers showed sufficient trust in him, nor affection for him. One day he thought that if he married into the Buddha clan, then he would become a relative and so Buddha would love him. With the object of securing a suitable bride, he sent his messengers to the kingdom of the Sakyas and demanded that a girl of the Sakya clan be given to him as a bride. The Sakyas were rated as Kshatriyas. The king of Kosala was not a Kshatriya but was a very powerful king and could not be denied. King Mahanama, the cousin of Buddha, had a daughter called Vasabhakhattiya born of a maid named Nagamunda. It was decided to give this bastard girl to Pasenadi. Accordingly word was sent to Pasenadi that the daughter of Mahanama, the son of Buddha's father's brother would be given to him. Pasenadi was pleased, but suspected some trick and said to his messengers: "Be very careful. These Kshatriyas are very proud and very cunning. They may palm off some girl as their daughter. Make Mahanama eat with her in the same plate and only then bring her as my bride." Mahanama pretended to eat from the same plate as the girl and so she came as the bride and became one of the queens of king Pasenadi. She gave birth to a son called Vidudabha. As this boy grew up, he noticed cer-

tain things and went to his mother. "Mother," he said,
"other boys are receiving gifts from their mothers' parents
and brothers; but your people have not sent a single gift
to me. How is that?" She soothed him saying that her
father's kingdom was far away off. The boy grew up to
be a young man and insisted on visiting his mother's
people. He started for the kingdom of the Sakyas with
a great retinue. The mother sent word to Mahanama
about the visit of her son. The Sakyas sent away all boys
and girls younger than Vidudabha to a distant part of
their kingdom and assembled in a border town to meet
the prince. The Prince of Kosala, as soon as he crossed
his kingdom, was received by the assembled Sakyas, who
introduced him to everybody and he had to bow down to
each one because he was younger than everybody. He asked if there were no younger people among the Sakyas (who
would have to bow down to him) and was told that because
of some illness the younger ones could not come. The
young man was feasted, made much of and loaded with
presents and returned. However, one of his retinue had
forgotten his weapons and went back to fetch them. He
went straight into the house where the prince had been
entertained and while he collected his weapons, he saw
a maid servant washing the wooden seat on which Prince
Vidudabha had sat. While washing the seat with milk
and water, the maid servant kept saying, "Oh, the pollution of the low born! It must be done away with." The
man slipped away quietly and told about the incident to
his master. Vidudabha made enquiries and in great
anger came back to his mother and beseeched her to tell
him the truth. Pasenadi drove her and the son by her
out of the palace, but Buddha argued with the king saying
that a son was a son after all and must be treated as such.
So Pasenadi reinstated the prince and his mother. The
prince in his heart vowed that he would wash his seat
with the blood of the Sakyas. After his father's death
he became the king and marched with his army against
the Sakyas. Buddha stood at the river crossing. Seeing
him, Vidudabha bowed to him and came back. Buddha

saved his kinsmen a second time, but the third time thought that he should not interfere. Vidudabha put to the sword every man of the Sakya clan that he could lay hands on. Only a few escaped. King Mahanama was taken a prisoner. After crossing the river Vidudabha ordered Mahanama to eat in the same plate with him. Mahanama asked permission to take a bath before eating, went to the river and drowned himself. So ended the Sakya clan.

In the same collection is related the story of King Udayana of Koshambi. In that story, Udayana's mother, a Kshatriya princess was lifted from the flat roof of the palace and dropped by a giant bird in the Himalayan forest where she hid in the branches of a tree. A man saw her and came to her rescue. He told her to get down from the tree. She declined, saying that she was afraid, he might be of a *jāti* different from her own and inquired who he was. He said he was a Kshatriya. She then asked him to show some secret sign so that she could be convinced. He did so and she then came down and accepted his help. The word used here is *jāti*.

The same commentary mentions certain streets as those in which only labourers lived.

In the Jataka-Katha a whole area is mentioned where only Vaddhaki (modern word *Badhai*—carpenters) lived.

Thus some centuries before and after the Christian era literature gives glimpses into a society, which was very much like the caste society of today. There were groups who had hereditary occupations, who married only among themselves, who probably lived in separate habitation areas, among whom there was hierarchy and some groups were even held to be untouchable. The stories told reveal attitudes and situations so surprisingly like those of the later days that one can surmise that the literature belongs to a society very similar to the caste society of the 19th and 20th centuries. Of the hundreds of parallels, I wish to point out only two. King Rajaram, the King of the Marathas, with a few faithful followers was fleeing away, hotly pursued by the Mughal army. In one town, the deferential treatment given to him by his followers roused the suspicions of the local Muslim officer. To convince him that the travelling companions were all of one caste and equals, Chitnis, a Kayastha, dined in the same plate as Rajaram, a Kshatriya. This incident occurred in the early 18th century. After the establishment of the British rule the main Maratha empire was dissolved, but a few feudatories were allowed to hold land and reign as Chiefs or Rajas. One of the more extensive and powerful of these "Indian States" or kingdoms was that of Gwalior, ruled over by the clan of Shindya with the title of Maharaja. The Shindya, though politically and economically very powerful, were held to be not Kshatriyas at all. Near Poona in the small town of Phaltan is a small chieftainship comprising of a few villages formerly ruled over by the clan of Nimbalkar Jadhav, which is supposed to be among the first five of the Maratha caste, which claims to be Kshatriya. I was recently shown some very interesting correspondence in which a situation, not unlike that of Mahanama Sakya is discussed. The Maharaja Shindya had a boy from the Phaltan Nimbalkars as his guest for a day. The mother of the boy has written the letter, suggesting what dodge could be used, so as to avoid eating at the same table, in the same row with the low-born Shindya. This incident occurred in the late 19th century.

CHAPTER III

INDIAN PHILOSOPHY AND CASTE

I have tried to show why I think that the full-fledged theory of caste very probably represents the working together into a single theoretical system two separate types of organization present in two societies. Through this formulation of the caste society, the two separate societies came to be represented as one society. Other aspects of Indian thought seem to be closely related to the society thus formed. Some of these are described here.

The Indian caste society was a society made up of semi-independent units, each having its own traditional pattern of social behaviour. This resulted in a multiplicity of norms of behaviour, the existence of which has found a justification in a religious and philosophical system. The separateness of the units was sought to be minimized by deriving all of them from four *varṇas*. In the religious thought a further remote unity was imposed on the *varṇas* by deriving them again from the different parts of the body of the primeval male[1].

In this social system the individual had no choice of behaviour. His norms were those laid down by the particular group to which he belonged. The castes were arranged in such a hierarchical order that at the top were the Brahmins, who were the most pollutable caste; at the bottom were castes whose touch—even the shadow—was supposed to pollute others. The caste in power tried to hold the lower castes to their lowly occupations and to the ritually impure position. There were authorities to legitimize the plurality of practices of the castes while holding the individual bound to the narrow groove set by

[1] *Ṛgveda* 10.90.

the caste. There were also features of the system itself which helped to support the system in all its inequalities. We shall consider these later. In this chapter I wish to discuss the ideal framework which seemed to give the whole system a certain logical consistency, providing an argument for its existence and continuance, providing a justification for its inequalities and at the same time holding out a hope for something better for those who suffered most under this regime.

Like everything else in India the completed conceptual system is made up of many strands of thought some Aryan, and some very probably belonging to the people whom the Aryans found in India. Some of these are traced below.

Philosophical speculation began very early in India. Already in Ṛgveda there are hymns about the rise of the world from nothing. There are the Aryan deities Mitra (the sun), Varuṇa (the god of waters), Indra (the king of gods), Agni (the fire), Ashwins (the twin gods) and many others. Gods like Tryambak and the mother goddess were added a little later and obviously belonged to the people among whom the Aryans made their home. It was apparently after taking up some new gods that a peculiar hymn came to be composed. This hymn has a refrain, "Which god shall we worship with offerings?"[2] The old gods, though many, had separate functions and rituals and had affinities among themselves; but when new gods came to be added, there was no special ritual for them and so possibly the question arose in the mind of some enquiring soul — "Which god shall we worship?" India was not unique in posing the question. A similar question was apparently asked also in the West, perhaps at about the same time by a king.[3] The answer given by this king involved choosing one god (The Aton) from

---

[2] *Kasmai devāya haviṣa vidhema.*

[3] Ikhnaton of Egypt ruled at a time when people worshipping Aryan gods and speaking Aryan languages had come in contact with the older civilizations of Egypt and Babylonia. These people were the Mittanni, Hittites and Kassites.

among the many.   The king failed in his attempt, but
the idea of one god being better than the others, of a
jealous god who did not brook the existence of other gods,
had taken root and later blossomed into three monotheistic creeds: Judaism, Christianity and Mohommeda-
nism.   The question, "Which god shall we worship?" was
never really asked, it was merely of a rhetorical nature. It
was answered on behalf of certain gods by their priests.
Each priesthood claimed its god to be not only the highest,
but the only true god. Christianity in its westward and
northward, march, abolished officially its rival creeds the
many gods of the ancient Middle East and of the Romans
and the Greeks and established one god and one church.
The West was set on a path in which it had to break with
its own past, deny its ancient gods and choose Christianity.
No question was asked about which gods to worship.   The
question was settled before it could be asked.   In India
the question was asked and the answers to it are preserved
for us in what are termed the six[4] philosophical doctrines
of India.   Each of the answers however is woven into a
complete philosophy of life and the universe.   The simple
question was almost forgotten in the larger issue, "What
is the ultimate reality?"   Curiously enough this search
again was not merely intellectual, but had the practical
aim of achieving happiness or bliss.   The final theory that
emerged had main elements which were common to the
orthodox Hindu philosophy and to the Buddhist and the
Jain philosophies too.   I will give here in a sketch the
conclusions as reached by the orthodox Vedanta school.

The early Aryans were afraid of many things.   The
chief among them was death and another was darkness —
the darkness after death, the darkness of night.   So this
new quest became a quest for immortality and light.   The
oldest literature does not have the idea of hell, though
the idea of heaven is found.   It speaks of realms of darkness or shadow.   Neither does the earliest literature

---

[4] *Shad-darshanas.* The four most famous of these are : Vedanta,
   Bauddha — the doctrines of the Buddhists, Jaina — the doctrine of
   the Jains, and Lokayata—the doctrine of Charvaka, the materialist.

mention rebirth. The idea of rebirth became definite before the idea of hell. It seems that this idea was not the original capital of the Indo-Europeans (Aryans and Greeks) at all, but was taken by them from non-Indo-European people. In Greece the idea did not become a part of the philosophical fabric as it did in India.

The Upnishads tell of the travel of the soul. In the *Aitareya* which is one of the older Upanishads, this travel is described until the seeker reaches Brahman.

The narration is almost in the form of an adventure story, where the seeker has to travel long through many obstacles. Then he comes to a lake, then he is asked certain questions, which when correctly answered, give him entrance to the holy place bounded by great Sal trees (*Sālajyam samsthānam*). There, sitting on a great couch, engulfed in light is *Brahman*. Here an old story form is used to describe an experience which cannot be described in concrete terms at all. At another place in the *Aitareya Upanishad* it is told how after death the soul goes up into the clouds to fall as rain-drops on earth and be born again when eaten as grain or grass by men or beasts. In this story a very old primitive idea is preserved in the formulation of the new doctrine of the transmigration of the soul. At another place the idea is expressed more forcefully without archaic accompaniments. The bodies are like dresses which the soul discards when they become worn and old, to don new garbs in the form of new bodies. This Upanishadic passage is found almost verbatim in the Bhagavadgita, which belongs to a much later period. Through the imagery of salt which dissolves in water, the idea of all-pervasiveness of Brahman is conveyed. One Upanishad (*Kena*) starts with a question, which embodies the daily practice of letting go of an arrow at a particular target.[5] "By whom impelled does the mind reach its object?" The whole sentence uses nouns and verbs which are generally used to describe the flight of

[5] Almost right up to and including the epic period, the bow and arrow remained the main and the favoured weapon of the Aryans.

H.S.—6

an arrow. The answer to this question contains the seeds of the theory of knowledge and the beginnings of psychology.

A third question akin to the question, "Whom shall we worship?" and "What is the ultimate truth?" was asked. It was, "What or who came first?" The question was answered in two ways. (a) Time (*kāla*) came first and time is the last. Time is the principle of change and movement and destruction; (b) desire (*kāma*) came first. Desire is the principle of creation and entanglement. These questions and answers are also very important as they form part of the full-fledged theory of Brahman. I have said that the quest of Brahman was also a quest for happiness. Happiness comes when a person is rid of all fears. An early Upanishad tells us, "One who knows the joy of Brahman does never fear". The story of creation is related at another place. Brahman was the one without anything else. It was lonely. It desired (*so kāmayata*) and through desire it became many. The word *kāma* has, throughout the literature, had a wider and a narrower meaning. *Kāma* means a desire, a wish, something one wants, just a general sense of wanting — a yearning. In the narrower sense the word means sexual desire. Thus in both its meanings it lends itself to the story of creation.

At about the same time another strain of thought was developing. This came out of the old practice of giving special offerings to gods in a ritual involving elaborate sacrifices. The word for this, besides *yajnya* (a sacrificial offering), was *ishṭi* (something desired). Different *ishṭis* with different rituals were practised apparently from very early times. We get for example instructions about the type of wood to be used for the sacrificial post depending on whether one wanted riches, food, progeny or heaven. *Karma* is a word used for all activity or work. This involves involuntary actions as also those prescribed by religion. Religious activities came to be divided into two main varieties : (a) *Vihita Karma* and (b) *Kāmya Karma*. The former was ritual which every person had to do at certain times of life and certain times of the day.

There were rituals at birth, puberty, marriage, conception, death. There were, especially for Brahmins, rituals for early morning, midday and evening. There was a ritual for certain days of the month and the year to give food to the dead ancestors. All this was prescribed necessary activity which ensured one's position in the early Aryan society. The non-performance of these rituals would lead to expulsion from the Aryan fold. In the early days it was not envisaged that there would be cases of deliberate neglect of these duties. They were a must.

The *kāmya karma* on the other hand was undertaken only on a special occasion and gave a man certain desired things. As already noted, this ritual was very elaborate and involved a person in much expenditure, which brought him fame as a rich man and as a generous donor. It became a matter of social prestige to engage in sacrifices which involved giving away of wealth.[6] Sacrifice always entailed the duty of feeding every person who came along. Sometimes it entailed giving to any person what he desired.[7] Besides *kāmya karmas* there were other types of actions which brought fame, merit and therefore heaven to men. These actions were feeding people and later, planting shade trees and digging wells.

Side by side with actions which gave positive worth to a person were actions with a negative content. Failing to do obligatory ritual or making mistakes in performing such rituals were such acts and expiation was prescribed for them. Failing to keep a contract with the gods was another. If you promised something to god in return for a favour and failed to keep up your part of the bargain, you would be visited by some disease. One such jealous

---

[6] The parallel to these is in American Indian Potlach. Kalidasa sings the praises of a king who was reduced to poverty through such a sacrifice. (*Raghuvamsha*, Canto 4). King Harsha is supposed to have given away everything he possessed in a grand orgy of *dāna* (gift-giving).

[7] The story of Astika who came as a beggar and asked that the lives of his mother's kinsmen be spared is told in *Mahābhārata*.

god was Varuṇa.[8] From very early times a distinction
was made between engaging in ritual and word-formulae
(sacred hymns) for procuring some good and engaging in
such activities to bring harm to somebody. The first type
of *kāmya karma* was "good". The second type involving
the killing of a rival in love, employing magic to bring
barrenness to a woman or disease to a man, etc., was "bad".
What is called black magic in the West is called *abhicāra*
in Sanskrit literature.

This early thought, which gave a plus or minus value
to certain actions developed into a general theory of action
(the *karma* theory), which says that almost every action
of man has a positive or a negative value. I have mentioned above that negative action is punished almost auto-
matically. This theory was also fully developed and
woven into the theory of rebirth, which in its turn got
worked into a full-fledged theory of hell and heaven, in
which there were many hells and many heavens. As
stated above, very few actions were without value.
Breathing in and out, winking of the eyelids, eating and
drinking, sleeping and waking, digestion and excretion
were actions which came nearest to being neutral, but eating and drinking were hedged in with taboos as regards
time, place and the type of food. Any breaking of the
taboos put a negative value on the action. Of the physiologi-
cal actions the sex act was the one most beset with taboos,
but *per se* it was not condemned and in certain contexts
was enjoined as a religious necessity. Only a son could
give food to the dead fathers (father and male ancestors)
and so one had to marry and beget sons. This world with
its actions and values was the world of attributes, especially three grades of attributes, the good, the medium and the
bad, and a summation of all actions at the end determined
the fate after death.

One more idea took a large share in the philosophy
that finally emerged. This again is an old thought pro-

[8] That this contract is still entered into will be apparent from Dr.
HARPER'S paper: Hoylu, *American Anthropologist*, Vol. 59, No. 5,
Oct. 1957.

bably belonging to the old Aryan *Kulturgut*. Day follows night to be followed by another day. Seasons followed one another and so did the months. The moon waxed only to wane again. All natural processes seemed to be in a cyclical rhythm. In Vedic hymns and later Brahmana prose literature the early poets voice their wonder again and again. The imagery used to describe this process is that of the moving wheel with six (seasons) or twelve (months) spokes. The rim of the wheel is also a geometrical figure (*chakra* — a circle) which has neither beginning nor end nor definite sides. This gave the idea of an infinite time, which has no beginning (*an-ādi*) or end (*an-anta*). The world moves on as a huge cyclical process without beginning or end. Death is followed by birth and birth has death as its constant companion. This idea is common to all three religious doctrines. It is a search to get out of this infinite cyclical process.

The Vedas with their hymns in praise and supplication of the many gods, the Brahmanas, with their sacrificial ritual, the Shrauta Sutras with directions for sacrifices, represent a literature which deals with the things of this life, tell one how to do good and avoid evil so as to prosper here, gain heaven and avoid hell. The *Upanishads* and the *Brahma Sutra* are books which deal with something which is beyond this world of (three) qualities. In *Bhagvadgita* it is said that "Vedas have for their subject matter all things having three qualities. Go beyond these, Oh, Arjuna". For this reason philosophical literature is called *Vedānta* (at the end of the Vedas). The philosophy is also called *Vedānta*. The final picture, as it emerged, was as follows.

The whole cosmos was conceived as being made up of many worlds peopled with many kinds of beings, each with its own life-span, many heavens one above the other, and many hells. The idea of hell as a place of torture seems not to have belonged originally to the Aryans. The earliest hymns talk about worlds, devoid of light, of beings committed to darkness. This conception with the very ancient ritual of periodically giving food to the dead ancestors seems to have analogies with the beliefs held by the other Indo-Aryan people. The idea of hell comes later and is first described in its fullness in Buddhist and Jain literature. The earliest texts do not have the idea well defined. It seems as if the Jains expanded and refined the picture of the hells. The heavens and hells were peopled respectively by different kinds of gods and suffering beings. Some of the beings peopling this cosmos are named — they are gods and demi-gods, humans who have become like gods, Gandharvas and Apsaras, the singers and dancers, the Yakshas, the Kinnaras and the Vidyadharas, living now on earth, now in heaven, different kinds of semi-human and human beings, all kinds of real and fabulous beasts, insects, birds, tiny life-forms which cannot be seen and plants of all kinds. This is the phenomenal world, where all beings act upon and react against one another; which feels, i.e. has sensations and emotions; which lives forever as a whole, but which is dying every moment as individuals. This world has moral qualities and attributes, has rewards and punishments and is founded in space and time. Nothing in it can occupy the same place, nothing can last eternally. The human beings and this world of ours belong here.

Above all this phenomenal world, including it, permeating it and transcending it, is the absolute being called *Brahman* (a neuter noun). This is thought of as a spiritual reality and in that context is called *paramātman* (the ultimate soul) as against the individual *ātman* (soul), which lives in the world of phenomena. The individual soul must wander through space and time, through many births, round and round in the great circle of phenomena (*samsāra-chakra,* or sometimes called simply *samsāra*) until it finds final release by the knowledge of its oneness with the Absolute Soul.

The theory then is as follows. The ultimate reality is *Brahman*. This is realized by a seeker in three stages which are given in three sentences in the Upanishads. The sentences are : "I am *Brahman*", "You are *Brahman*", "Indeed, all is *Brahman*". This means that everything

that is, is *Brahman*.   Does it mean that *Brahman* is merely another word for the totality of the phenomenal world?
No, definitely not.   The phenomenal world is bounded by
time and space.   Everything in it has a beginning and an
end and is at a particular place.   It has also qualities like
red, white, smooth, rough, cruel, kind, good or bad.   The
Brahman is infinite, eternal and above all qualities, but at
the same time all the phenomenal world is its manifestation.   The analogy given to illustrate this point is :   "A
ripple on the ocean *is* ocean, but does not exhaust the
ocean."

The conception of the Ultimate Reality has very important consequences.   The *Brahman* is the source of all
phenomena but is itself beyond it.   The human world with
its descriptive and normative constructs does not represent
ultimate reality because there is an infinity of other worlds
with their objective and value structures and all those are
also emanations of *Brahman*.   A few examples will make
this clear.   Time and space concepts are relative to the life
experience of each type of being.   For a human, whose
only means of locomotion are his legs, two points on the
opposite sides of a canyon mean a descent of, say, a mile,
a walk on the valley bottom and an ascent of another mile.
To a bird the distance is but a few furlongs, to a worm
crawling slowly along with its world confined perhaps to
a few square yards the other side of the canyon is beyond
thought.   The same is true even to a greater degree of a
tree fixed at one spot.   In the same way time is different
for different beings.   The old writers were never tired of
inventing stories to illustrate this point.   In *Bhagavadgita*
we have the following verse[9]: "The day of god, Brahma the
creator (not to be confused with Brahman), is equal to
1000 times the four *yugas*, the night is of the same duration.   *Chaturyuga* (the 4-*yuga* group) is made up of
12,000 years of the gods.   Each year of the gods equals
360 human years.   So in one day of Brahma there are

---

[9] *Bhagavadgita*, 8th Canto, 7th verse.   Also A. L. BASHAM, *The
Wonder that was India*, p. 321.

thousands of years of gods and millions of human years.
What is a day for the creator is years for the gods and
aeons for human beings. This reckoning is rather abtruse
but it is used again and again to emphasize the momentari-
ness of the human world. The same point is brought forth
vividly in many stories of which one from Buddhist literature is given below.[10] A god with his retinue of beautiful
women was amusing himself one day in a heavenly garden.
One of the women climbed a tree to pluck fruit, fell down
and died. She was reborn on earth as a girl, married when
she came of age, had children, lived to a ripe old age and
died, to find herself opening her eyes surrounded by that
god and her other friends. The god said to her tenderly,
"My beloved, it took us quite a few minutes to bring you
back out of your faint". She laughed and told him what
had happened to her during those few minutes and on hearing her experience, all wondered at the shortness of human
lives.

Just as time and space are relative, so are all phenomena relative. What you see as a particular colour changes
with the change of light or with a change in your organ
of perception.[11] Gods all share in this relativity. All the
worlds from that of the trees and the insects to that of the
humans, all the heavens and all the hells are but different
aspects of *Brahman*, the Absolute. Each is relative. Each
taken alone is false.

This conception leads to the thought that the world of
human values — the most dearly held of human posses-
sions — has no absolute reality and that everything being
a manifestation of Brahman has a right to exist. This

---

[10] *Dhammapada, Aṭṭhakathā.*

[11] The ancient Indians would have been delighted at the new discoveries, which give us a glimpse of the world as seen by other
creatures, e.g., the honey-bee. The bee has a different visual
spectrum from ours. It cannot see our reds, but sees ultra-violet
as a colour and perceives polarized light, which we cannot per-
ceive at all. (See the work of VON FRITSCH, translated by Dora
ILSE). In the same way, bats hear supersonic waves which are
not heard by us as sounds at all.

thus is the source of and the justification of the continuous and simultaneous existence of a multiplicity of behavioural patterns in the Indian society. The typical
Western reaction to this doctrine can be found in recent
(1960-61) articles in "Encounter" magazine by Arthur
KOESTLER. An idealist who has deeply imbibed the three
monotheistic creeds of Judaism, Christianity and Com-
munism and who has always thought 'Good' and 'Truth'
to be one, cannot but feel impatient at a doctrine which
refuses to call 'evil' evil. The doctrine does not deny moral categories in this world, but emphasises that what we
call "values" are "human values" and that they have no
relevance beyond man and his society. KOESTLER's criticism of Zen Buddhism is also unwarranted because it
teaches a doctrine about ultimate reality. The *māyā-vāda*
of Shankara has also lent itself to both angry and facile
criticism. These doctrines need to be studied historically
and critically. They are not formulated as an answer to
any particular crisis, personal or global, though one may
find a mode of dealing with both on the strength of the
knowledge of these doctrines. Before one can understand
them one must cease quarrelling with oneself and the
world.

Shankara in his writings recognizes and gives a name
to two types of truths. One is the absolute truth (*pāra-
mārthika satya*), which has no limitations of time, space
and attributes. It is one. The other truths are many, are
partial. He calls such a truth the truth of daily intercourse (*vyāvahārika satya*). These are truths which have
a validity for the world of behaviour. When a blind man
describes his world, it is a world of touch and hearing and
smell and that world picture has a validity, for it suffices
for the behavioural universe of the blind man. What is
true of the blind man is true of all creatures of heaven and
earth.[12] However endowed these creatures may be, their
endowments will always fall short of the totality which is

[12] See in this context G. K. CHESTERTON's poem which tries to describe
the world of a dog.

Brahman and its creation.[13]   This point is well brought
out by Dnyaneshwar, a 13th century Marathi commentator
of the *Gita* (this is the usual way in which the *Bhagvad-*
gitā is referred to in India).   As pointed out above,
Brahman is described in two ways.   One way is to deny it
all attributes or give it contrary attributes.[14]   The other
way is the more popular way, well known from the earliest
Vedas.   *Brahman* is described as a MAN with thousands
of feet (feet everywhere), thousands of eyes (eyes
everywhere), thousands of hands, thousands of heads.
Dnyaneshwara's commentary on this verse says : Whatever action there is among the smallest and the largest is
his action.   He is everywhere at all time and so he is all-
foot.   All eyes everywhere are his eyes and so he is all-
eyes.   He is all-head because not only is he all but like the
head he is above all.   All sound is his word, all that hears
are his ears.   He has all forms because all that has form
is his manifestation.[15]

Indian philosophers are fond of stressing that
Brahman, the Absolute, is found in all creation from
Brahma (the creator) to the small ant.   This all inclusive-
ness is reflected in what I have called a culture by accre-
tion.   It includes and accommodates.   It rarely rejects.
Among all Indian philosophers there is no dichotomy of
good and evil because all is the manifestation of *Brahman*.
As the Absolute is above all attributes, all moral categories

---

[13] I am grateful to Prof. R. D. VADEKAR and Prof. P. L. VAIDYA
for drawing my attention to the following passage from The
Madhyamaka Sutra, a Buddhist work ascribed to the 4th century
and so pre-dating Shankara by at least 3 centuries :
"The Dharma-teaching of the Buddha is based on (the recognition of) two truths, one the truth that covers the world
[the later Māyā-doctrine of Shankara], and the truth that is
ultimate".   *Vide* : Buddhist Sanskrit Texts, No. 10, Chap. 24,
p. 215.

[14] The description in *Ishopanishad*: "It goes, it does not go; it is
far, it is very near; it is within all, it is outside of everything"
or the famous description: "It is not that; it is not that" (*neti;*
neti).   Also *Bhagavadgitā*, 13th canto, 15th verse.

[15] *Dnyaneshwari*, Canto 13, verses 74 to 86.

belong to the world of partial truths. By the very nature of things there cannot be anything which is absolutely final. Neither heaven nor hell are final stages. The ethical world, the world of values, becomes a world of relative truths under this view. This conception of the universe is so relativistic that it should lead to a society which is anarchist — a society in which agencies of control other than an individual's own would be absent. But the Indian society is governed by rather strict rules of behaviour. These rules are the rules of the group called castes, though some rules govern the behaviour of all, to whichever caste a person belongs. The caste society is arranged in a hierarchical way. The family also is arranged on principles of precedence, obedience and subservience. How can such a society be explained by the theory described above? As already explained, the Hindu society has two aspects. One is the co-existence of groups with different norms of behaviour and a continuity with the past and the second aspect is the structures which govern behaviour among co-existing groups called castes and among families within each caste. The first aspect is explained by the theory of *Brahman*, the second aspect comes within the orbit of what is called the theory of *karma* which is as follows :

Life is an eternal process involving birth, death and rebirth. All types of life — sometimes even non-living matter[16] — is linked together in this process. A human being after death may become a denizen of heaven or hell or may take an animal shape or become a tree. What sets this wheel in eternal motion is *karma* — action. As explained previously, according to the Hindu view (Jains and Buddhists also shared it), every action of a human being has a positive or a negative worth. At death there is always an accumulated capital of positive values and negative values and the soul must pay for both. The account is never made up in such a way that a positive value

---

[16] A person can become an inanimate thing for a certain duration and then assume a living form. In this context the story of Ahalyā in *Rāmāyaṇa* is interesting though it does not illustrate the cycle of rebirths.

can cancel out a negative value. The soul must receive
the meed for both. Thus one and the same being can live
in heaven for some time and in hell for some time for the
good and the evil one has done and be born as a human
being to start the account over again. The type of status
in which a being is born in human society also reflects the
award of positive or negative worth, which is not all exhausted by heaven, hell or non-human births. A man
being born as a king or a Brahmin is a sign that there
was an accumulated plus balance, being born a member
of a lowly caste or of vicious parents is a sign of a minus
balance. Thus on this theory the caste society with its
hierarchy, social differentiation and social injustice found
its justification. The distinction between castes was felt
like a distinction between different types of animals like
lions and foxes. Being born in a low caste was merely
a special case of being born as some other being.[17] There
was however a great difference between being born as a
human being, however lowly in status, and being born as
an animal or even a god. The different kinds of birth
as heavenly beings or animals, plants and beings in hells
are called collectively births of reckoning or experiencing,
(*bhoga-yoni*). In these births a being is incapable of ac-
cumulating positive or negative worth. He merely lives
on his capital of good or bad. It is a passive living out,
but when the capital is exhausted, one is born again as
a human being to start on a new birth where he has a
choice either to gather a plus capital or a minus capital,
in which case he is born again, or, he may refuse to gather
any capital — to end with a zero — and be gathered into
the great *Brahman*. The human birth is the birth of
action (*karma-yoni*).[18] Whatever position one may
occupy in human society, there was the choice one could
exercise of the paths to (1) heaven, (2) hell or (3) non-

---

[17] See Appendix to chapter 2.

[18] This is quite clearly stated in all Hindu, Jain and Buddhist philosophical literature though some of the story literature of all three
suggests that positive or negative action is also possible in other
births.

rebirth and incorporation into *Brahman*. The *karma*-theory thus justifies the caste society and at the same time offers a hope for the future. The kind of behaviour which leads to heaven or hell is described as follows: Doing good to others, feeding the hungry, not stealing, not coveting the other man's wife are the usual good actions. To these are added: feeding Brahmins, showing due respect to elders and above all *doing without a murmur all the jobs incumbent to the station in one's life* (*this includes the work expected of a caste*). On the other hand, stealing, adultery, treason, cruelty to man and beast and insubordination to elders and *towards those of higher castes* led to hell. What is then the path which leads to the ultimate release from the cycle of births and union with *Brahman?*

Very peculiar strains of thought have gone to make the complete theory of *karma*, which is not all of it given in one place. The total picture is quite clear, but it is not brought into one system in one discourse. This theory of *karma* is bound up with a theory of *dharma*. *Dharma* is a very peculiar word. It has two aspects, one naturalistic and the other normative. In its naturalistic meaning *dharma* means a necessary attribute. It is then a synonym for such words as *svabhāva* or *prakṛti* (own attribute, nature). For example the *dharma* of water is to flow. In its normative meaning, which is the one used oftenest, *dharma* means "the duty, the path to be followed". In discussion after discussion *dharma*, the duty, is made to follow from *dharma*, the natural attribute. In this context, the word *"vrata"*[19] and its history is also very interesting and reveals the evolution of thought. *Vrata* seems to be used as synonym for the word "path", the way, in *Rgveda.* It is used especially for the eternal circular paths followed by the great luminaries. To go by one's *vrata* was the duty of each. *Vrata* was then used

---

[19] V. M. APTE, "All about *vrata* in Ṛgveda", *Bulletin of the Deccan College Research Institute*, Poona, Vol. III, June 1942, and W. Norman BROWN, "The basis for the Hindu act of Truth", *Review of Religion*, November 1940, Vol. V, No. 1, p. 37.

for the chosen way of life, but it was also used for the 'natural' way of life. In *Rgveda* there is a song which tells how each follows his *vrata* devotedly and has desires which go in accordance with his *vrata*.[20] "A carpenter, following his *vrata*, wishes for a break in a chariot, a surgeon wishes for a maimed one, a Brahmin for a patron who will engage him to press soma, the sacred liquid. . . . In the same way (equipped) with wood (fuel), bird's feathers (for dusting), stone (an anvil) and flames (fire), a goldsmith seeks out a man who has gold to be worked."

"I, a poet; my father, a surgeon; my mother, milling grain; we with different thoughts, as we seek wealth follow each our *vrata*, as a herdsman follows his cows. In the same way a draught-horse desires a chariot easy to draw . . . . the phallus desires a hairy cleft (woman's organ), the frog desires water".

Vrata was first a path, then a function chosen or a natural one. Being a poet was a chosen vocation. Being a frog or a draught-horse or a phallus was having a natural function.

This word is compounded with others to show a type of virtue. *Anuvrata* was a person who stuck to his functions — duties. *Satyavrata* was a person whose duty was his truth. *Pativratā* was a woman whose *vrata* was her *pati*, husband. Just like *dharma*, *vrata* had a naturalistic and a normative meaning. In the earliest literature it means a duty, a vow undertaken. In later literature it means a duty incumbent on a certain position in life. The duty of a woman was to be *pativratā*. The duty of a Shudra would be to serve others, the duty of water or a river would be to flow.

Certain actions were called good or bad, but very few actions were good or bad for all. Manu says, killing is sinful, but it is the duty of a king to order an offender to be killed. Neither the king nor the hangman would be committing a sin if they killed through a sense of duty. Each person had a duty (*dharma* or *vrata*) appropriate

---

[20] *Rgveda*, 9, 112. See reference above, W. Norman BROWN.

to his station in life. Following this duty did not enmesh
a person in a cycle of births or deaths if it is followed
without mental involvement. Such a way of life makes
a person possess extraordinary powers (*siddhi*) which are
otherwise acquired only by sages and ascetics through
meditation and penance. This point is illustrated in a
Buddhist story, which is about *Satya-kriyā,* an act of
truth. This consists in doing something extraordinary
through certain powers of truth. In performing such an
action one has to make a declaration publicly or mentally
about one's steadfastness to "truth". The most famous
of such examples in Indian mythology is that of Sita.
When Rama expressed doubts about her faithfulness, she
declared, "If I have not sinned against my husband by
word, deed or thought, may mother earth take me in".
The earth opened and took Sita. In this way Sita proved
her innocence. The Buddhist story, which is very illu-
minating in the context of *dharma* and *vrata,* as the duty
imposed by the station in society, is as follows :[21]

---

[21] This passage is quoted from W. Norman BROWN, loc. cit.

In this context the following story from *Mahabharata* is re-
vealing (Āranyaka Parvan, Adhyāya 197-206). A holy Brahmin
sitting in contemplation under a tree was spattered with excreta.
He looked up in great anger and saw a pair of birds which at
his look died instantaneously. He then started on his daily round
to beg food in the city. He came to a house and called loudly
that he had arrived. The housewife who was cleaning the pots
asked him to wait. In the meanwhile the husband of the woman
came home. As soon as she saw him, she left her work, washed
her hands, brought food for the husband and while he ate stood
by him talking sweetly and serving him. After the husband
had eaten she remembered the Brahmin standing outside and
came out hastily with food, begged the mendicant's pardon and
asked him to accept food. The Brahmin in a rage abused her
and enquired if she thought it proper behaviour to keep a Brahmin waiting. She replied calmly that as a married woman her
first duty was to her husband and a Brahmin should not get
angry and go on killing birds. The Brahmin was surprised at
her answer and begged to know further about duty and meri-
torious life. She had no time but directed him to a butcher
living in the kingdom of King Janaka in the city of Mithila.

"King Ashoka inquired if anybody in his kingdom would perform an act of truth. No Brahmin or monk or Kshatriya came forward to do it. At last a courtesan, Indumati by name, came forward and before the assembled multitude made the mighty river Gangā flow upstream. After witnessing this astounding feat, King Ashoka said to her, "You possess the power of truth! You, a thief, a cheat, corrupt, cleft in twain, vicious, a wicked old sinner, who have broken the bonds of morality and live on the plunder of fools!"

"It is true, Your Majesty," she answered "I am what you say. But even I, wicked woman that I am, possess an act of truth, by means of which, should I so desire, I could turn the world of men and the worlds of the gods upside down".

Said the King, "But what is this act of truth? Pray; enlighten me".

The Brahmin walked for days and on reaching Mithila was directed to the butcher's shop. He stood apart but the butcher saw him, hurriedly stepped down, bowed at the feet of the Brahmin and took him home. After worshipping him the butcher told him about his killing the birds and his conversation with the dutiful housewife. The Brahmin was astonished and asked how a man doing such work could have such spiritual achievements. The butcher replied, "What I do is because of the deeds of my past birth. I can't help it. But I do it from a sense of duty only. I serve my parents and gods, give to Brahmins and live without untruth and cruelty". Then follows a long discourse on how everybody must do what has been accumulated through deeds of the last birth and how one could still be released.

The moral is obvious. Despised beings like women and Shudras (the two are always bracketed together) can get extraordinary powers and attain Brahman — realisation — provided they do their traditional work in a humble spirit, with a sense of duty, rather than for self-aggrandisement. Arjuna's business as a Kshatriya was to fight and provided he did it purely from a sense of duty and not to enjoy the status of a king, no blame attached to him. Traditional behaviour was thus raised to the highest moral principle. A person was born in a particular status because of his own deeds and the best could be achieved by him doing things which were done traditionally by people in that rank.

"Your Majesty", whoever gives me money, be he a noble (Khattiya, i.e. Kshatriya), or Brahmin or a merchant (Vessa, i.e. Vaishya), or a serf (Sudda, i.e. Shudra) or of any other caste soever, I treat them all exactly alike. If he be a noble I make no distinction in his favour. If he be a serf, I despise him not. Free alike from fawning and contempt, I serve the owner of the money. This, Your Majesty, is the act of truth by which I caused the mighty Gangā to flow upstream."

The teaching of *Bhagvadgitā* is to be read in this context. The stanza most often quoted says, "It is better to die in (performing) one's *dharma*. The *dharma* of others is fearful of consequences."

"Even if one's *dharma* seems mad, its performance brings blessing, rather than the taking up and following another's *dharma*"[22]

In the following passage the word *karma* is used as a synonym for *dharma*.

"Men obtain great *siddhi* (power or ultimate release), when they remain immersed each in his own *karma*."[23]

The words *"sve sve karmaṇi"* (in one's own *karma*) can be substituted by the words *"sve sve dharme"* (in ones's own *dharma*) in this passage, as it is done in the following verse 47.

This theory of action, though abstruse in parts, has direct reference to the Hindu social structure, as we shall see. As noted above, good and bad actions do not cancel one another to make a zero; therefore, each action has to become a zero, i.e., a perfectly neutral action from the point of view of value. This is possible only if desire is given up. Desire flows from the conscousness of "I" as distinguished from "the others". This ego-feeling is at the bottom of desire and all desires lead to actions towards fulfilment. There is no point of satiation at which desires die through complete fulfilment.[24] Thwarting of desire

---

[22] *Bhagavadgitā*, canto 3, verse 35.
[23] *Bhagavadgitā*, canto 18, verses 45 to 47.
[24] *Manusmṛti*, 2, 94; *Bhagavadgitā*, canto 2, verses 62, 63.

leads to anger, anger leads to temptation and madness
which lead to destruction. Intense love is also a path of
destruction. Love blinds no less than hate. Love leads
to attachment and desires and endeavours on behalf of
the loved ones. Complete release can come only when one
is without hate or love.[25] The very beginning of the wheel
of life and the phenomenal world was in the desire felt
by *Brahman* "to be many". To be completely neutral is
the goal. The illustrations given for this type of behaviour are those of the sun, the water and the earth. The
sun shines on everything. He does not say, "I will give
no light to the wicked". The water does not say, "I will
quench the thirst of a cow, but shall become poison and
kill the tiger," nor does the earth say, "I shall support
the great and banish the lowly."[26] So must a person act
if he wishes to obtain final resease. *Whatever position he
is born into, he must fulfil the functions, but without attachment, without hatred.* If he does live in this way,
neither sin nor merit attaches to his actions.

We thus reach a rule of life in which each fulfils the
duties of his station in line without resentment.[27] If one
dies without any longings, or desires, one realises *Brahman.*
The king becomes the upholder of the social order. His
function is compared to that of the god Vishnu, whose duty
it is to keep the world in a state of being. He is the god
of the *status quo.* The king fulfils this duty. He holds

---

[25] The story of Ananda, the most devoted disciple of Buddha, points
out this moral. Ananda once asked Buddha why many other
disciples had been released but he had not received salvation.
Lord Buddha answered, "My dear Ananda, I will tell you when
the right time comes."

  When the Lord Buddha was on his death bed, Ananda immersed in inconsolable grief was sobbing his heart out. Then
the Lord Buddha called him and asked "Ananda, why are you
crying ?" "How can I live without you, my Lord ?" replied
Ananda.

  "Now you know", said Lord Buddha, "why you have not been
released."

[26] *Dnyaneshwari,* canto 12, verses 144-150.

[27] *Bhagavadgitā,* canto 4, verse 20; also canto 5, verse 10.

the balance between the castes and does not impose laws of his own; he administers them.   Manu says that the king shall administer justice so as not to go against what is appropriate to a country (*desha*), the time (*kāla*) and the caste (*jāti*).   He is not a law giver.   He is simply the upholder of a system and that system is the caste society. Thus whether it is ultimate release or heaven which one strives for, the actions to be performed are the same.   The one set of actions, i.e., those that lead to release, are done without any ultimate individual aim, the others which bind, are done for the sake of gaining a good name, wealth or power.

Brahman, the Absolute, in its totality is amoral.   The act of creation is not a moral act.   It is a natural consequence of desire.   To the question, "Why was this world created?" the answer is, *"Just play-activity"* as in the case of human beings"[28]   Moral action can arise only through intercourse and in society where individuals and groups interact.   Therefore in the moment of the ultimate realization of *Brahman* one rises above all social laws, but yet one must behave as if one still 'belonged' to society because, "the common people imitate the actions of the wise and great and your actions should serve as guide to people."

The principal guides to actions were Shruti (the Vedas), Smṛti (the books written by Manu and others) and Vṛddhācāra (the behaviour of the elders).[29]   The

---

[28] *Shankarbhāshya, Brahmasutra of Badarayana*, 1.1.33, "*Lokavattu Lilakaivalyam*".

[29] The word vṛddhācāra does not appear in this context in Sanskrit literature. It is found in Marathi literature of the religious sect *Mahānubhāva* and is used in conjunction with the words *Shruti* and *Smṛti*. In Sanskrit literature however the expression *vṛddhānuśāsana* (the advice of elders) occurs in *Mahabharata* (*Nalopakhyana*, 13.17). The expression *anādi-vṛddha-vyavahāra-paramparā* (the ancient tradition of the behaviour of the elders) occurs while defining the language of ordinary usage (*laukika-bhāṣā*, KAIYATA'S comment on *Mahābhāṣya*), and lastly *āchāra* (customary behaviour) is defined as "the acceptance of that which is said by the elder (or the teacher)", occurs in *Sarvadarshana Sangraha*.

Vedas being ritual books never provided real guides for what was *dharma* or *karma*. The Smṛtis, were rules of behaviour, as 'remembered' through tradition, but they could not be infallible, because societies are forever in flux. The most reliable guide was, therefore, the example of the elders, the respected people, who know what was appropriate to the time, place and caste in the light of Shruti and Smṛti.

An individual was born with three debts (*Rṇa*). The debt to the gods, to the preceptors and to the ancestors. The debt to the preceptors is paid in the first part of one's life (first stage of life) by learning the lore and the traditions of the *varṇa*, the debt to the gods is paid by worship, by feeding the hungry and sheltering the needy. All this can be done only through marriage and keeping house (second stage of life). The debt to the ancestors is paid by continuing the line, having sons and giving food to the dead ancestors (second stage of life). After discharging these debts one can retire from active life and stay away from the daily duties of a householder (third stage of life). After a few years, if one feels that way, one can deny completely all claims of society and give up everything by taking up *Samnyāsa* (casting everything off). This is done by performing publicly one's own funeral ceremonies, taking up another name and giving up the house and family, (fourth stage in life). In this stage a man belongs to no caste and all caste rules for him cease to be.

Paying the three debts, following the tasks appointed to one's own caste, without hope for bettering one's lot or resentment or despair at life's reverses, recognising that this life is the consequence of all past actions and going through it with equanimity, one at last reaches *Brahman* and realises that one is *Brahman*, the one is many, the Eternal-in-Flux.

This in short is the philosophy which brings the caste society into a conceptually connected structure. The questions asked at various times receive answers. One of the questions asked again and again in early literature was about creation. Various answers were given on the basis of analogy and myth, but as the *Brahman* theory reached its culmination, the questions lost their interest. The world of phenomena as manifestation — a play-activity — of *Brahman* is eternally destroyed. The creation and destruction are but partial views of an incomprehensible eternity.

The question, "Which god shall we worship?" also loses its importance. Gods as against the *Brahman* are as phenomenal as everything else. Man creates gods in the necessity of his own desires. In the *Bhagavadgita* Krishna, the god, says, "I take different forms according to the different needs of my devotees.[30] A 17th century Marathi poet Tukārām says, "God! Have you forgotten that your godhood depends upon our belief and devotion?"[31] The minute a man realises, "I am *Brahman*," he is above all gods. There are and will be always many gods because men's wishes will be many.

The question about what is right and wrong were answered in different ways depending upon the circumstances. Theoretically, right and wrong were not absolute. Practically right and wrong was decided according to the general principles of *dharma* as modified by principles of time, space and *jāti*.

This system was completed in its main features by the epic times. The history of India shows that all the kings, native or foreign, did rule according to this theory, allowing each caste to rule itself and a group of castes to accommodate themselves mutually, provided the taxes were paid to whomsoever was the ruler.

---

30 *Bhagavadgitā*, canto 4, verse 11; canto 7, verse 21.
31 *Tukaram Bovachya Abhanganchi Gatha*, (Marathi), Vol. II, verse 2946. Bombay, Government Central Press, 1950.

Chapter IV

SOME MECHANISMS OF THE CASTE SOCIETY

In the caste-society separate units have lived together for a very long period. Some questions naturally occur with regard to this society. How and why could such a society continue to exist for such a long time? What were the modes of articulation of the units called castes? What constituted the "togetherness" and the "separateness" of these units? What advantages did such a society offer and to whom? Or what did such a society lack? Was the "separateness" of castes complete or was there communication between castes? What were the processes of communication leading to imitation of behavioural patterns? What are the limitations on imitation? What were the modes of changes in such a society? How did they come about? I am attempting to indicate the answers to some of these questions in this chapter.

How and why could the Hindu caste society endure for a long time?

Certain features of the caste society, for example the multiplicity of behavioural patterns, hierarchy and hereditary social position found a full rationalization in a very elaborate philosophy which included a theory about final liberation. However close the fit of the theory to the Hindu society, it cannot fully account for the long existence of such a society. The philosophical speculations were themselves the product of the long existence of such a society. A society does not exist simply because its structure justified it on ideal grounds. There must be some other reasons for the continued existence of an elaborate social structure like the caste.

Before taking up that question one point needs to be mentioned. The existence of a social system which perpetuates great inequality in status, worldly goods and opportunities depends among other things not only on the acquiescence by the non-privileged groups but also on a feeling in the higher groups that they have a right to rule. A certain legitimization of power is necessary to hold up those groups which enjoy a privileged position. Slavery was condemned not only because it became economically untenable, but because the group represented by the exploiters of slave labour did not feel justified in using slave labour. The "White man's burden" was not merely a hypocritical and high-sounding phrase coined to garb naked exploitation. It represented the belief which sustained the empire builders in their conviction of being a people with a mission. The same type of thought helped the proselytising Christians in the spread of Christianity in Europe and then in the world. In the same way the religious and philosophical system of Hinduism, besides being a speculation about the nature of the world of existence and the world of values, was also the source which upheld the caste system and the privileged ranks. It answered the need of the higher castes to justify their existence and to legitimize their exploitation of the caste situation. It must be borne in mind, when systems of beliefs linked with social institutions are studied, that in any social situation the class which rules and controls needs self-justification on ideal grounds as also mechanisms which make it possible to rule and control. The ideal system of beliefs and speculation has already been described. In this chapter an attempt is made to study the mechanisms of the system which have enabled it to survive so long and in doing so to find if some of the questions asked at the beginning can be answered satisfactorily.

The history of India is not so well known as the history of Western Asia and Europe. The chronology and dynastic lists are not always well authenticated. For certain periods and for certain areas there are gaps which have not yet been filled. But while the record is unsatisfactory in details, it is adequate for certain purposes and lets one draw certain broad generalizations. One such is that peo-

ple have come into India continuously from outside for the
last three or four thousand years. From the conquest of
Alexander till the coming in of the Western Europeans the
record for two thousand years is quite clear. Every few
centuries different folks and tribes came into and settled
in India. Each ruled for some time to be overthrown by
indigenous rulers or some new comers. After Alexander,
some of the people who came into India and ruled bigger
or smaller kingdoms were the Greeks, Persians, Shakas,
Kushans, Huns, Tartars, mixed Turkish-Tartar people and
various other Central Asiatic tribes. The long border between Tibet and India has always been open to a continuous
trade between Tibetans and Indians and a number of people from over the border have come and settled on the
Indian side of the Himalayas. The greatest pre-Alexander
immigration of which we have knowledge was that of the
Aryans. They formed part of the great southward thrust
over a very wide area from the Mediterranean to the
Himalayas of a horse-riding, cattle-raising people of mixed
origin. These people were first heard of around 2000 B.C.
in Egypt, Babylonia and on the upper reaches of the Tigris
and Euphrates. They ruled as foreign barbarians in
Egypt (Hyksos) for centuries and were driven out after a
great effort. They ruled in Babylonia (Kassites) also for
centuries and were gradually absorbed into the people and
took over the culture of the people among whom they lived.
In India there did not appear to be the kind of well-knit
civilization of long standing as that in Egypt and in Western Asia.[1] But apparently there were great walled cities
in the Punjab and Sind where people lived a life comparable to that lived by the city dwellers of Babylonia.
These people were apparently in touch with the western
civilization, but who they were is not known as their script
represented by words on various seals has not been de-

---

[1] Modern excavation shows that the city-civilisation of the Punjab
was very extensive and also well-knit, but the exact pattern of
its intercourse with people inside and outside India is not yet
revealed. See *Indus Civilization* by Sir Mortimer WHEELER, 1960.

ciphered yet. This civilization was destroyed, whether by the Vedic Aryans or by some other people is not known. In the Vedas there is a mention again and again of a warrior God (Indra) who is often described as the smasher of cities. The name of this god occurs in a treaty signed between an Egyptian Pharoah and a Mittanian king at about 1500 B.C. The Aryan record in their earliest hymns and epics is one of fighting with various indigenous people and establishing small kingdoms. We may presume that various people, perhaps related linguistically to Vedic Aryans, came into India over a long period, that other people also must have come into India besides the Aryans and that the history of the two thousand years before Alexander's advent into India was not much different from that of the two thousand years after Alexander. What kind of society there was before the Aryans came we do not know, neither do we know much about the adjustments which took place each time between the new comers and the older inhabitants. We do know however as to what was happening in a general way after the Aryans arrived and in a more detailed way at the time when Buddha lived. In a previous chapter I have tried to give some reasons why I think that a society somewhat like the present caste-society might have existed even before the Aryans came. The Aryans had a society different from the caste society, but they gradually accommodated themselves to the caste society and finally tried to theorize about it. After Buddha, when we get numerous descriptions of the caste-society, we know how its very self-sufficiency made it indifferent to who the ruler was to whom certain taxes had to be paid. A little later we get the picture of the caste-society working in a spatial unit called "a village" (*grāma*). The interdependence and mutual need of castes became perfected in the village organization.

"Arthashastra" (300 B.C.) of Kautilya describes a village as a walled settlement. Though the number of open villages is large today there are traces of walls in many. In a modern Indian village different castes live in different localities. Within each area representing the clusters of houses of one caste, there are sub-clusters belonging to particular families (agnatic lineages and sometimes an affinal family or two) within the caste. A caste has an area of distribution comprising many villages. Within this area a man finds all his kinship. Families belonging to a caste are residents of certain villages. In each village families of each caste form certain patterns of give and take with all the other castes. The village together protects itself and pays certain dues to the ruler. During famine or war or owing to oppression by rulers whole villages may migrate. It was in the interest of the ruler not to tax these self-sufficient communities too much.

The caste society, each unit-caste of which was rather helpless economically, became a powerful self-regulating system through being organized into villages. A foreign ruler could rule provided he did not disturb this society very much. As long as there were officials to collect revenue and command compulsory services on some days of the year according to customary procedures, the villagers did not care whom the official represented. This was an easy society to rule. All that a conqueror had to do was to establish his rule in the capital city and go on ruling as those before him had done. No new governmental machinery needed to be set up in such a society. This society had brought to near perfection a mode of self-government which needed the least supervision from a central power. The caste had a cell-like structure, but for subsistence as a caste it needed a certain type of contact and give and take with people of other castes. A village was an almost perfect cell as an area of sustenance which was self-sufficient, independent and isolated from others through its very individuality. In the village the articulation of each caste to the others became defined and through this was developed an amazing system of self-regulation which needed almost no central supervision and withstood all central interference. The regulation was local and atomic. The caste society had two kinds of structures which cut across each other without coming into conflict. The principle of regulation of the caste from within was the principle which held together and regulated kin. This involved the localized patrilineal or matrilineal family (joint or non-joint) living under one roof, the lineages living as neighbours and the whole web of blood and affinal kinship was represented by caste. The father of the family, the most important members of the most important lineages and caste-elders were the centres of authority. The village represented the system by which intercaste intercourse was regulated. A village in itself, though atomic and self-sufficient in one sense, was part of a larger system of villages dependent on one market town or representing areas of the spread of particular castes or families. The conduct within the village, between villages and between a village and the authority represented by the political power was regulated through the agency of the village council. This society made it easy for any conqueror to rule provided that conqueror was content to rule according to traditions.

This historical picture and the kind of organization which faced the Aryan immigrants and became strengthened in time contrasts greatly with what was happening in Europe. The Indo-Europeans penetrated Europe which was still largely inhabited by fishing and hunting folk and had made beginnings in agriculture. It absorbed this element, dominated it and submerged it so completely that only traces of the culture of the pre-Germanic people remained. After the overrunning of Europe by people speaking Indo-European languages the main land-mass of Europe remained undisturbed by foreign conquerors. The Huns penetrated the south and later the Mongols and Turks penetrated upto the Elbe and the Danube but the rulers of Western Europe remained largely native rulers. The most important factor in European history was the gradual spread of Christianity from the south to the north. Christianity had at its back the civilization of the great Roman Empire. The Empire fell but the Church carried on its tradition of law, organization and centralization. It supplied a central point of reference for all conduct, it alone sanctioned norms of behaviour. It cannot be said that it was a rule of enlightenment which fought superstition and ignorance. India in those early centuries presented a picture of greater enlightenment, liberality and less superstition. What the Church did was that it had a hegemony of thought. Beliefs sanctioned by it alone could be held so that the ignorance and superstition were also of a uniform brand. When this power of the Roman church was shaken after the Renaissance, the bulk of superstition and ignorance could also be removed. In India each caste and each village was a separate centre of power and ignorance and superstition. Political instability and chaos were certainly endemic all the time in the sense that in one area or another there was an overthrow of a kingdom and every area had it at least a dozen times during the known history of India. The caste society was so constituted that it could withstand the shock of such events and offered a certain amount of security[2] to individuals and families.

---

[2] The extent and quality of protection offered by the caste (which I have defined as extended kin) can be judged from the following two examples. Some years back the Deccan College, Department of Archaeology was engaged in doing excavations at Nevasa a town about 120 miles from Poona. The labour employed for digging etc. was all from the scheduled caste 'Mahar'. When the excavations were over these people mourned the end of the work. They said that from the next year they would have to migrate as usual after the rainy season in search of work. Enquiry revealed that most of them went to Poona and lived during this period at the houses of their relatives.

   The second time this was brought vividly to the notice of the author was during the recent (July 1961) disaster in the city of Poona. Two dams broke after a month of incessant rains. On the 12th of July the city was hit and laid low by millions of tons of water and subsequently for two days it had no water to drink. A daily newspaper ascertained from the railway and bus transport authorities that about 100,000 people left Poona to go to different places in Maharashtra. This figure was arrived at by counting the tickets sold. These people did not go to hotels but to their relatives. A relative is not a member of the near family but may be any relative by blood or through marriage. From those whose houses were submerged about 25 per cent sought shelter in public places. At one

It is not generally realized that the caste society in a sense was a very elastic society. It has been pointed out how each new group could become a part of the caste society in whichever way it chose or in whichever way historically accommodation became possible. By its very nature the caste society presented a loose structure which could take on new units and in so doing re-arrange old units. It could do so without having to change the very nature of the society. Different tribal people became articulated to the caste-society in different ways. Some became an integral part and assumed the position of the untouchables (Chenchus), others or rather parts of others claimed to be Kshatriyas (Raj-Gonds and ruling Bhils), some remained occasional visitors to the settled caste-society as organized in villages (semi-nomadic castes of entertainers), some foreign people got completely absorbed (the Gujar, some Huns, etc.) while others remained on the periphery (the Parsis and the Bene-Israel Jews of Bombay). The caste-society had become such a strong habit of thought that even egalitarian religions like Christianity and Islam became organized into caste-societies. The Brahmin-Christians married only Brahmin-Christians and in South India low-caste Christians were not allowed to enter a church for purposes of worship. Rajput-Muslims married only among themselves.[3] The caste society perfected a mechanism by which groups lived juxtaposed without actual mingling or losing their identity, which demanded specialization and economic interdependence, which gave security and order without assistance of a central machinery. The caste as a kinship group and the caste society as organized in the village were both largely atomic structures sealed off from other similar structures. The internal control was within the kin group called caste

place were people belonging to an untouchable caste whose whole settlement was submerged. About 75 per cent of the people were sheltered with people of their caste and kin.

The author has known a case in which a family of Rajput-Muslim refused to have an untouchable Hindu as a household servant because they as Rajputs could not tolerate it.

and the control and rule of conduct, where it came into
contact with other castes, was for all practical purposes
determined within the narrow sphere defined by the limits
of a village. This mode of life in two intersecting isola-
tions was so pefected long before the Christian era that
later history had to make accommodation to it rather than
that it could get modified in response to demands of
history.

In India, the easternmost country in which the Indo-
Europeans penetrated, the picture was different from what
happened to them in western Asia as already noted above.
There were a few cities with a little writing, there was
agriculture, there were other ruling people and the earliest
records of the conquerors show that they were neither
much superior nor inferior in civilization to the people
among whom they came. The only advantage they possessed was a great mobility. The cities knew writing but
it was apparently very meagre and they were destroyed
either by the Vedic Aryans or by their predecessors. The
life of the cities reveals trade and specialization. The
Indo-Aryans were neither submerged nor were able completely to dominate. The author thinks that they accommodated themselves to a life which allowed a certain
separateness together with a certain interdependence — a
pattern which very soon became what is known as a caste-
society. One can contrast this picture with that in Europe
where Christianity imposed a certain fundamental uniformity. It could do so because Europe was a comparatively backward region while Christianity had at its back
the whole ancient civilization of the Mediterranean world.
By the time the Christian Church started on its path of
domination of Europe and suppression of older religions,
India had started out on a diametrically opposite path of
accommodation, and inclusion of ever new elements. The
philosophical ideas of the ultimate truth being *Brahman*
and all else (including gods) possessing but relative truth
was well established before the birth of Christ. In this
society, the extended kinship group, the family, the caste
and the village (the local unit) remained far more im-

portant than the state, while an organized church never emerged. Each group lived near others, keeping to its own traditions while co-operating with others in the matter of production of consumable goods. The society which developed was of an agglomerative character. This character is developed to its fullest extent in the organization of castes. Simple agglomeration is a process which needs the least modification of the agglomerating units. The new element which is being incorporated is simply joined and it can remain in an unspecified position for a considerable time. This makes it clear why a new group coming into a region can remain for a long time in the position of a semi-absorbed caste. The Jews, Parsis and a number of Muslim castes in various villages, while fulfilling very important economic functions in the life of the village communities, have an indeterminate position as regards caste hierarchy. The very principle of articulation of castes is thus characteristic of the whole Hindu culture. The agglomerated or conglomerated mass of matter in geological or physical terms has no definite internal structure and no definite limits of accretion of new matter. The caste-society is however not structureless. A rough scheme of meaningful differentiation in terms of rank and obligations has during history been imposed upon it. There has remained a certain indeterminateness as regards rank and the obligations and duties *vis-à-vis* other castes. In any given region, the number of castes may vary and the position occupied by different castes may differ widely from region to region. The *varṇa* system embodying a ranking order was imposed on this mass of agglomerated groups in such a way that theoretically at least the castes of any region fell into four divisions. If we count untouchables as a separate category it would make five divisions. Within each of these five divisions, there were innumerable groups each striving for a higher position within the *varṇa* division. Today there are a number of castes in the three *varṇas* who claim a position which is not conceded to them either by the *varṇa* where the group wants to be, nor by other *varṇas*. The castes within a *varṇa*, though showing great rivalry among themselves, sometimes show solidarity while fighting for position against others. Thus at all times Brahmins of whatever caste may work together to substantiate the claim of belonging to the highest *varṇa* and to keep out the new aspirants from entering their *varṇa*. Even this position is complicated by the fact that groups within a *varṇa* may be historically affiliated as mutual friends or champions of castes of lower *varṇas*. This is the position in Andhra with two sets of castes. The higher castes are the Reddi and the Gauliga. These two caste sometimes claim to be Kshatriyas. They are traditional rivals. The Reddi are on terms of friendship and patronage towards an untouchable caste called the Mala, while the Gauliga are on similar terms with another untouchable caste called the Madiga. The Mala and the Madiga proverbially hate each other. We have here the picture of complex alliances and rivalries within the *varṇa* and between *varṇas*. Similar observations have been made about conditions in Malabar (Kerala) by Mr. Raman Unni.[4] He notes (p. 520) that the "Chaliyans, originally an immigrant caste of weavers ...... are now regarded as a low caste of Nairs". The same author also observes that in another group of villages the ranking of immigrant castes is vague (p. 329). At another place he describes the attempt of a lower caste (Variyar) to rise higher in temple service through the influence of Nambudri Brahmins.

In the same way, sometimes the actual numerical strength of particular castes plays a role in the eternal struggle for power. A traditional ruling caste, whose numerical strength is somewhere between 40-50% of the population might find itself being opposed by 10 or 12 castes each of which forms a numerically small minority, but which can combine in a successful opposition to be able to wrest certain concessions from the ruling caste. This happens especially in modern times

[4] Ph.D. Thesis, Baroda University, 1961.

where every adult has a vote. The principle of agglomeration becomes gradually modified. Many castes live
together in one village and can join and rejoin in a struggle
for power. In Maharashtra, e.g., one particular caste may
numerically be the majority caste. One finds therefore a
tendency for smaller castes to go away from the village
and settle in small market towns, which serve the needs
of between 20 to 40 villages. In such a market town the
traditional rank would no longer count and castes which
were considered to be lowly or which were numerically
small could combine to get power. The amount of definite
configuration which can be imposed on the simple agglomeration of a caste society depends on cultural communication in its widest sense. The communication is the
knowledge and acceptance of certain structures involving
acquiescence in values and positions of subordination and
domination. In India the most widespread item is the
large knowledge of the *varṇa* system. Even though the
word *varṇa* may not be known to the illiterate masses, the
rough classification and the words Brahmin, Kshatriya,
Vaishya, Shudra and untouchables are understood by
almost everybody. The Brahmanical order of ranking
which places the five divisions in a descending order in
the order given above is also known to most people, but
is not acquiesced in by large sections of castes belonging
to groups other than Brahmins. Historical records show
that this struggle for acquiescence is a phenomenon which
goes back to the first written records of Hindu society.
Every branch of Indian literature has preserved stories
of rivalries between different *varṇas* especially those
between Kshatriyas and Brahmins for supremacy of
position. The position in this respect has always been
one of constant friction with opportunistic accommodation. This pecular conflict though theoretically confined
to two *varṇas*, really reaches to all people in all *varṇas*
inasmuch as there has been all the time an attempt by
different castes to claim being Kshatriyas or Brahmins.
As northern domination reached all parts of India, the
varṇa system came to be established as a theoretical point

of reference throughout India. The attempts of castes
to rise ever higher in a hierarchy are never with reference
to single caste position, but always with reference to
varṇas. When a Kunbi of Maharashtra wants to call himself a Maratha, he is not changing his caste name, but his
position from the Shudra *varṇa* to the Kshatriya *varṇa*,
because in historical times the Maratha caste has successfully claimed to belong to the Kshatriya *varṇa*. The
varṇa system also changes internally. Different groups
through their claims to belong to a higher *varṇa* all the
time upset the established ranking system. But it remains
fixed in the sense that all concede that there are five ranks.
Until recent times, the divisions at least were held to be
the ultimate divisions of society. Even when the Brahmins and Kshatriyas have fought for supremacy there has
been a reluctant admission of the theoretical highest position of the Brahmins at least as regards ritual. The fact
which we note when we come to analyse the system of articulation of different castes in different regions of India at
a given period or at different times in the same region is
that the *varṇa* system which appears so inflexible itself is
surprisingly flexible, because while the words denoting the
five orders remained the same, the castes included in them
changed. Brahmins being the literate class, who have
written most of the systematic literature about law and
ritual, have given always the impression of a certain inflexibility to the *varṇa* system, which in actuality has not
been the case. With regard to the question of wielding
power and exercising social control and dominance the
varṇa system shows even a greater indefiniteness than the
Brahmanical writings would lead one to expect. Indian
history is full of names of big and small rulers belonging
to all sorts of *varṇas* holding sway over bigger and smaller
regions and exercising control over castes belonging to
higher *varṇas*. Sometimes the first rank allowed to a
Brahmin is nothing more than a matter of form and lip
service, while real power and control vested in whoever
happened to be either the political head or the rich man in
a given village.

The degree and the quality of separateness or together-ness of groups which make up a society are difficult to judge purely from the way the groups are structured and articulated. As long as the norms (within certain elastic limits described above) are undisturbed, even an extremely differentiated society involving discriminations due to rank may present a picture of unity and happiness. In such a situation a lowly servant willingly gives up all for the sake of the master, or a caste bows down to the fact of being regarded as untouchable. Culture-contacts, new technological discoveries, disintegration due to prolonged wars might lead to new economic opportunities or to up-heavals leading to a new social order. On such occasions the tenuousness of links becomes demonstrable. The feel-ing of togetherness is also due to spread and depth of com-munication. It is best to examine this point in some de-tail as regards the caste and village society. Togetherness may even emerge in an age-long institutionalized rivalry as between Brahmins and Kshatriyas where, as already shown, the rivals in one context become allies in another. This is exactly the picture which the caste society presents. It is an ever-changing pattern of alliances and rivalries. What castes will gang together and against whom, depends on the particular internal structure of the system, as also on the outside historical situation. The foreign mission-aries and rulers tended to patronise the lowlier and more deprived castes who found novel and undreamt of opportu-nities under the new set up.

The *varna* scheme into which all the hundreds of castes were fitted was generally known all over India long before the Christian Era.[4] The greatest supporters of that system were the two top *varnas*, namely, Brahmin and Kshatriya. They were rivals of one another but also at the same time useful and indispensable to each other. Southern kings from very early times claimed descent from the legendary heroes of the Sanskrit epics and Brahmins

See mentions of *varna* in later Vedic hymns, Mahābhārata and all the Smṛtis.

supported these claims.   As representatives of the kings of
the north they were the supporters of the *varṇa* system and
with it, we may presume, of the *jāti* system.   The doctrine
of rebirth was part of all the three religions (Orthodox,
Buddhist and Jain) over hundreds of years.   The doctrine
that the present birth was a consequence of the deeds of
the past births was equally well established.[5]   This has
been considered in some detail in chapter III.

The notions of heirarchy and pollution and also the
relation between a low birth and the sins committed in a
former birth were communicated to the populace in various
ways.   All the three sects had a host of itinerant holy men
who told people stories to illustrate certain doctrines.   The
same notions were repeated in dramas acted at great
temple festivals which drew a crowd of the same type as
the temple festivals do today.   The types of discourses held
by the Buddha are vividly depicted to us.   The intinerant
monks in their hundreds must have held similar discourses
all over the land.   In a drama of the 7th century[6] which
notes that a Shudra had no right to perform penance of
the Brahmanical times, the first act vividly tells us the way
in which the drama was acted.   There was the festival at
the local temple of Shiva.   A company of actors had arrived with a new drama by a not well known man.   An actor
apparently stood on high and drew the attention of the
people and described the work and the play commenced
with the words, "Now, folks, I have become a citizen of

[5] In Bhagavadgita, Arjuna asked anxiously, "supposing one were
to die while making efforts to reach the ultimate release, without
attaining the end, what happens ?   Are all efforts lost ?   Is one
to begin all over again ?"   Krishna answers that one starts in the
next birth in a position where one is advantageously situated for
carrying the efforts further and assures Arjuna — "Do not be
sad.   You are well born (*abhijātosi*) to a status where you enjoy
goodly virtues."   The term *abhijāta* is never used of people born of
low caste.   In the same way the words of Krishna "I have created
the four *varṇas* according to the nature (of people) and works
(of people)" can also be construed to mean deeds resulting in a
low birth.

[6] BHAVABHUTI, *Uttara-Rama Charita.*

Ayodhya of those olden days." Thus the communication of the ideas making up the caste system reached to all levels of the population through Sanskrit and different types of Prakrit.

Between the 10th to 12th century, the modern north Indian languages gradually emerged. Of the Southern Dravidian languages, Tamil and Kannada were very well established. The first literature in these languages was bringing into vernacular the thoughts in Sanskrit literature. The thirteenth century literature shows all the above ideas incorporated into Marathi and Gujarati. The communications became even more effective as they were in the regional languages of the people. Mutually understandable communication in a language which was not just the language of the learned had many consequences. (1) It imparted the ideas of the caste and the high philosophy of the Sanskrit treatises to the masses. (2) it coincided with a new religious movement offering salvation to everybody and (3) It fostered a feeling of togetherness among those who spoke the same language.

Panini's Grammar and later Prakrit works make us realise that even before this period Sanskrit was spoken in slightly different idioms in different parts of India and that different types of Prakrit were spoken in different parts of India. But the emergence of the modern languages marks a definite stage in the social history of India. Politically a region speaking one language may have been governed by more than one king, but for social intercourse of all types the linguistic region became a new consolidation. At the same time it separated the other linguistic regions to a certain extent.

The type and form of communication within each region has remained the same over centuries and the names of some types of communicants from the Maharashtra region are given here as an example.

1. *Haridas* — these are generally Brahmins who go from place to place and give a performance in temples in which the deeds of god and his greatness are sung. Such

a performance is half music, half prose, half story telling
and half hymn singing. It is a one man act.

2. *Puranik* — is also a Brahmin who is generally
attached to one place and who tells the stories and lore in
the Puranas every day in a temple.

3. *Gondhali* — is a troupe of non-Brahmin performers of a certain type of devotion involving song and story.
They are intinerant. There are others who tell the philosophy of the Gita.[7]

4. *Chitra-Kathi* — are also non-Brahmin itinerant
story-tellers who illustrate their stories with pictures.

5. *Yama-puri* — (the city of hell) is a performance
given in each big temple festival. This illustrates the kind
of tortures suffered by the sinners in hell. Little dolls are
used in this performance while a man goes on giving un-
interrupted commentary all the time. It is avidly visited
by adults and especially by children.

There are also other entertainers who get on the move
after the rains and visit villages. There are astrologers,
snake-charmers, magicians, medicine-practitioners and all
types of performers. They are all on the move as soon as
the roads become dry and the harvest comes near. Though
the village people are comparatively immobile, the communicants are all very mobile and cover great distances
reaching even forest-villages.

The festivals of local deities and great all-India deities
are also occasions of very active communications.

It is the experience of the author that among the illiterate people of Maharashtra, there is far greater knowledge
about the literary tradition of the last seven centuries of
this land than among the people who have received their
education in schools and colleges. There was thus effective communication of the fundamental theoretical framework underlying the social structure. As all the rulers
and their Brahmin priests supported this structure, there
was enforcement and to a certain extent acquiescence in it.

---

[7] Some ten years ago a man popularly called Gita-Maharaja was
giving lectures on Gita in the city of Nagpur. Over five thousand people listened daily to these discourses.

Communication leads to imitation. Imitation brings about certain uniformities of behaviour which help the feeling of togetherness. In this respect communication has played a very peculiar role in India. There are certain uniformities which are found over very large regions. These uniformities embrace all castes. One such uniformity is language. The sameness of language facilitates communication and imitation. The author has noticed many examples of this type of communication. A number of castes which did not allow cross-cousin marriage allow it as a concession to the majority pattern. In a non-compulsive social set up such communication and imitation is almost the only force for achieving certain uniformities. The working of this seems to depend on many factors. Some castes seem to resist change for a long time, others seem to accept change rapidly. The duration of association, the types of association, the rank of a caste, all seem to have an influence on the phenomenon of change, its quality and its intensity. A type of imitation is called by SRINIVAS "Sanskritization." In his field studies he has noted that certain people from a lower caste try to imitate the habits of speech, dress and food of higher castes and so try to rise in status. Besides raising status, this type of imitation also leads to establishment of certain uniformities. But the experience and historical studies of the present author have shown that the process of "Sanskritization" by the very nature and history of the caste society has very severe limitations and must be interpreted in a way different from the role attributed to it by SRINIVAS.

In certain respects castes distinguish themselves from one another very sharply and some of these distinguishing marks are valued as caste-monopoly. Characteristics based on sectarian differences or tribe-like distinction are almost never imitated by well-to-do individuals of the lower stratum of castes to emulate the rank of the higher castes. In an orthodox setting such behaviour may not be interdicted as long as the man of the lower castes preserves his distance; but the author has seen that such individuals are the butt of ridicule and contempt instead of praise from

their fellow caste-men as well as from men of superio
castes. It is recorded in history and literature that cer
tain things were forbidden to people of certain castes an
that contravening of this taboo was severely punished
Vedic learning, practice of penance, wearing Brahmanica
apparel were the things tabooed. Certain foods were als
tabooed to certain castes. These taboos became slack a
well as unenforceable under certain historical circumst
ances. Those were also the times when some aspects o
the caste order came to be challenged as the history o:
Buddhism, Jainism and the Bhakti movement shows
The taboos and their severity became very slack during
and after the British period. During this period the
author has noticed again and again that a conscious imitation of the dress or accent of a higher caste is something
not looked upon with favour by many lower castes. Ir
this respect the marriage of a man of a lower caste to a
woman of a higher caste has two aspects. Some tend to
view it as a matter of triumph while others view it as a
betrayal of the own caste.

Imitation is a process which affects the imitator as
also the people of other castes. Certain types of ritual are
performed generally by higher castes. Some castes whose
position is disputed may also perform the ritual. In such
a case the Brahmins who cater to the priestly needs of the
lower castes lose status within their own caste.[8] There
are some types of worship which are performed both by
higher and lower castes, but the Brahmins who are employed by the lower castes lose rank within their own
caste. This fact illustrates the double role of the imitative
process.

Generally the times when caste-taboos get less rigid
are during foreign rule and intensive culture contact. In
India this was provided almost all the time by the contact
or conquest both externally and internally. At such times
new castes claimed and reached the Kshatriya rank. It
cannot be said however that imitation preceded the gaining

[8] One can interpret this phenomenon also as a failure to attain
Brahminhood.

f a rank. In many cases the claim to a rank precedes mitation. Successful imitation becomes possible only after claim to a higher rank is made good.

The mechanism of imitation as a factor towards social hange is, in the Hindu setting, a very complicated process nd its possibilities and effectiveness seem to be enhanced n the very circumstances when it seems to be not necesary.

The feelings of togetherness engendered within a caste nd within a village are complementary in the sense that he sphere in which one type of togetherness works is lifferent from the sphere of the other type of togetherness. The caste bond is primarily a kinship bond and ometimes holds on even when occupational or religious lifferences occur within a caste. Generally when people hange over to another religion, the caste bond breaks as narriage ties are broken. But the author has seen cases especially among the untouchable castes when families keep in touch even after conversion. There are cases of narriages among converts and non-converts. Sometimes nembers of one and the same family may belong to lifferent religions.[9] Occupational differences do not affect he solidarity of a caste ordinarily except as it introduces great economic distinctions. The togetherness of a village lepends on long residence of different families which are pound in a certain pattern of services and duties and which are known one to the other. This togetherness is expressed in Marathi by the expression *"Gāvachā* (of the village) and *Uparā* (a stranger). The author found that people whose families had lived in a village for two generations at least would be called *Gāvachā*. In one investigation carried out by my colleague Dr. Damle, it was found

Such cases were noted by the author among the Mahars of Maharashtra. In the tribal area such cases were noted among Bhils in the Khandesh district of Maharashtra and in some Munda villages in South Bihar. A similar situation was reported to the author by one of her Sikh students. A number of families had Sikh and non-Sikh members in the Punjab before the present tension due to the Punjabi language area arose.

that a man who had lived in a village for over ten years
was called *Uparā,* and treated as a "stranger" in certain
critical situations. A man for some reason falling out of
his own village community could hope for support from
his caste people settled in other villages, but if a caste ex-
communicated a man, it would have been very difficult for
any village to give him support.[10] In a village people supported each other against extortion from the central
government. In a famine whole villages migrated as ever
Buddhist records show. A village gave fight to the robbers. We have a poem from the late 18th century which
illustrates the feeling of togetherness rather well. A
Brahmin poet MOROPANT from the town of Baramati near
Poona went to Benares on a pilgrimage. In a poem ad-
dressed to the holy river Ganga he has pleaded the cause
of his fellow-villagers and begged the river to wash their
sins. In this poem he has mentioned by name: Brahmins
Marathas, Vanis, Kumbhar, Parit, Lohar, Sutar, Barber
and the untouchable Mahar of his little town.[11] Even the
Muslim is mentioned. This is one aspect of togetherness
but in certain other aspects togetherness did not exist at all

The concept of "togetherness" has significance on
various levels of experience. This feeling may bind people of a locality or of a larger area. It may bind people
over large time-spans. The spatial and simultaneous "togetherness" depends on various factors like long and continuous communications as also on common dangers and
common oppressions, common beliefs and common political
domination. The feeling finds, linguistic expressions as
Gāonwālā or *Gāvachā* ("belonging to the same town") as
we have seen. Other linguistic expressions may refer to
political oneness, or linguistic oneness[12] or religious one-

---

10 Excommunication is legally banned in India now.

11 *"Ganga-Vakili"*, *"Moropanta-Krita Sphuṭa Kāvya"*, edited by
    Vaman Daji OKA, 1896, Part I, pp. 57-63. I am very grateful to
    Prof. T. S. SHEJWALKAR for bringing this poem to my notice.

12 Poets of Maharashtra have given expression to this togetherness
    e.g. *Marāṭhā titukā meḷavāvā"* (All Marathi--speaking people
    should be united together).

ness.[13]   The possession of a family name, clan name or a
caste-name may also express the feeling.   In trying to
assess such a feeling or the lack of it the historical behaviour of a society is the best guide.   Some aspects of
such behaviour seem to be implied in the very build-up of
a system.   The stresses and strains of the system seem to
be understandable from the way the parts are arranged
and articulated.   The caste rivalries and alliances are
thus a consequence of its hierarchical order.   At the points
of stress and strain certain securities against snapping
seem to be built up in the value system or moral and religious beliefs and on the systems of reward and punishment
of temporal and non-temporal nature.   But the capacity
of a system to withstand strain or to build in securities can
never be fully known for a system which goes on living,
because what the future strains would be and how a society will meet them is largely a guess based on its past
performances.   Each society has a capacity for change
which may surprise and also give a new insight into its
nature.   The systems of a vanished society can be fully
analysed but even then one cannot say that it had inevi-
tably reached the point of breakdown.   The breakdown of
a particular society is a historical event.   One can analyse
the factors leading to it but rarely can one say that a
breakdown was an absolute logical necessity and was inevitable.   "Might have been" is a phrase every historian
toys with and without it a social analysis might become
merely the laying bare of fatality.   A 'breakdown' is also
in most cases a relative breakdown.   When the conditions
of disturbance vanish it is found that in its rebirth a society carries certain continuities with its past and as long
as such continuities exist there are always the possibilities
of revivals, and resumptions of old forms of behaviour.
'Togetherness' encloses different circles of people in different contexts.   Shared knowledge and experience does

---

[3] Expressions of religious oneness so common to the West occur
in Buddhist or Jain literature in earlier times and in the later
sectarian Hindu literature.

not necessarily lead to a feeling of togetherness. European
wars of the last thousand years were fought between
Christian countries, but Europeans as a whole tend to have
the "us" feeling against non-Europeans and Christians
against non-Christians. Conflicting situations may arise
in these two loyalties especially since a certain new political dogma has led to a schism in European society. Thus
European and non-European Christians may join against
European and non-European communists who had tended
to dissociate themselves from Christianity. This is a
picture of a society[14] which has first consolidated itself
through one religion, then in smaller political national
states and lastly through a consciousness of being different
from the rest of the world, which was simply a world for
exploitation. Common resistance was made to Muslim
domination through the symbolism of the Crusades and
through the real persistent fight against the Moors in
Spain. The Mongol invaders of Europe turned back for
some reason from the eastern bank of the Elbe. This
incident has been treated by European historians almost
as god's grace and the triumph of the Greeks over the
Persians as an act of god which preserved the fine classical
tradition for the future of Europe.

A glance at Indian history, the actual behaviour of the
people and the tone of the historians show a great difference in attitude. From very early times, people of
various racial stocks and various religions came into India,
fought whoever was the reigning king in the region they
came to, established kingdoms, and perished in their turn
to give place to new kings. This process continued right
up to the recent past with a very few exceptions. The
Rajputs fought against the Mughal rulers of Delhi but
never as a whole people. Some kings fought while at the
same time other Rajput kings were vassals and allies of
the Mughals. The Marathas and Sikhs fought against the

[14] European society in this context includes the American society
which is an overflow of the 'European' society. It excludes
Asiatic Russia as it was a sphere of mere colonial enterprise
throughout the European Russian domination.

Muslims but the Maratha resistence ceased after a time.[15]
The only time that India fought as a whole against the
foreigner was during the struggle for freedom against the
British. This went against all historical precedents and
must be counted as an achievement of the British Imperia-
lism. The complete organized mastery of the foreign
power led to a new organizational orientation for this land
which never before then had felt to be one politically.

What holds for political power holds for religious
organization too. The loose religious beliefs which formed the core of Hinduism were without a name until one
was given by the Muslims. The term "Hindu" was coined by Muslims and gave a new consciousness of one-ness
to people who were so designated. Hindus remained
separate from the Christians and Muslims mainly because
the two latter refused consciously to accommodate to the
Hindu pattern of life. Even so the Hindu pattern imposed itself on these communities inasmuch as the converts
assumed or rather carried over into the new life the old
habits of thought by keeping ideas of caste and pollution
in the new religion. Even those who were not converts
but original Muslims and Christians succumbed to the
idea with the result that a *varna* and caste-system parallel
to the Hindu system arose among them. The white Christians were the Brahmins in the new caste system while
the untouchables converted to Christianity had to stand
outside the church for worship. The picture was further
complicated by the mixed progeny of the whites and the
natives whose position in the new caste hierarchy was the
most bitterly contested. The same phenomenon was seen
also among Muslims. However, the two religions, through
their more formally organized priesthood, retained the
possibility of assuming a common feeling of togetherness
among themselves and a feeling of separateness from the

[15] The spirit in which Shivaji fought or the spirit in which the
battle was continued till the death of Aurangzeb was lost in
the later years when Marathas were content to acknowledge the
nominal suzerainty of the Moghul king and made him a pawn
in a complicated political game.

infidel. This contact with the uncompromising monotheistic religions made Hindus more aware of themselves
as an entity than at any former period in the history of
India.

The feeling of togetherness through time is not a
feeling shared equally by all. In Hindu society while there
is much change, nothing seems to be finally given up, with
the result that there is always some living link with the
past in some aspects of behaviour and thought. The
Hindus have been called an unhistorical people who have
never kept clear chronological records of anything; but
they have kept a continuity with their own past in behaviour and thought which is not found in the lands of the
West. Christianity in Europe and Islam in Western Asia
have cut up the experience of these societies into two
separate epochs, one before the acceptance of the new
religion and one after the acceptance of the new religion.
The pre-Christian symbols and beliefs are matters of anti-
quarian interest and evoke no feelings in the present generation. The recall of the past becomes a romantic revival.
In India there are people who carry on even today the
ritual of three thousand years ago in a language which
is as ancient. The traumatic experience and the split
personality with its guilt feeling, whch the Western world
has, has been largely absent in India.

Another aspect of the measure of togetherness and
separateness can be realized through certain recent occur-
rences. Almost all over India conversion was going on
in Muslim times and later after the Western Europeans
reached India. The converted Muslims became castes and
performed hereditary functions in villages becoming an
integral part of the village-economy. The phenomenon
of conversion was very wide and intense in certain parts
of India like Sind and Eastern Bengal where between 75
and 50% of population became Muslim. The converted
population went on doing the same jobs they were doing
before conversion. The fact of conversion did not evoke
fear or anxiety in the minds of the non-converted upper
castes. Hindu society made up of many castes functionally

interdependent had in reality become lop-sided in these two areas without anybody becoming aware of it. These two areas became part of the new Muslim State at the time of partition and the full separateness or the superficial togetherness of the old caste society divided by religious beliefs became apparent.

It was stated above that the organization, unity and all-pervasiveness of the British rule led to a new feeling of togetherness among the Hindus. This feeling was continually put to test especially in the relationship of the untouchables castes with the rest of the Hindus. The untouchable castes tried to improve their social position by using political pressure. There were bitter accusations by their leaders against the high caste Hindu leaders, and by the high caste leaders there was criticism of the attitude of the untouchables. But on the whole the untouchables cast their lot with their countrymen against the white rulers. The pressure of conversion to Islam and Christianity was always very great. In this context their recent *en masse* conversion to Buddhism needs to be studied as a gesture of togetherness coupled with a strong protest against felt social injustice.

Closely related to this aspect of togetherness is also the question of the offence and defence mechanisms of such a society against aggression. It has been pointed out above that in its long history the Hindu society as a whole never rose as one (except recently against the British) against political, cultural or religious aggression. The fact however remains that while the more centrally organized societies of the west succumbed to political and religious domination to a degree intensive enough to change radically their structure, the Hindu society has survived over two thousand years of continuous pressure from foreign conquerors and new religions. The survival became possible through its very structural looseness. Its weakness seems to have proved its strength. It is recorded in European history that the conversion of a king or queen has led to the conversion to Christianity of a whole land or a whole people. This was never the case in India.

The political power from the earliest times was divorced entirely from religious functions and Asoka the Buddhist king could not convert even the majority of his subjects to Buddhism.   He had to give recognition and protection to other sects.   The Hindu society could not be attacked as one.   If one part succumbed, it was cut off while the rest of the society went on in its old unconcerned way. Well-knit 'togetherness' transmits feelings of resentment against transgressors.   It becomes everybody's business to be his brother's keeper.   That was exactly what the looseness of Hindu society prevented.   Its tolerance was but another   name   for   the   indifference   of   one   part   to the fate of the other.   This was also its defence.   If one part was lost, the rest of the society did not feel the shock. One attack is not enough to conquer such a society.   The attacks have to be as many as there are loose parts.   In the last analysis these are the innumerable castes and sometimes even families within each caste.

This type of organization is comparable to the organization of the worm's body which is made up of semi-independent segments.   If a segment is cut off the rest of the worm goes on living.   The death of the worm can be achieved only if a large number of segments are destroyed. This is what happened in the case of East Bengal and Sind.

The phenomenon of change in this society has also been in keeping with its character.   It has changed in some aspects, while in others it has not changed at all.   Some parts have changed while others have remained practically unchanged.   Its attitude to change is also different from the one found elsewhere.   Brahmins used to eat beef as is clear from the Vedic texts.   For over a thousand years they have given up the old practice.   Beef became taboo to almost all Hindus, except to the untouchables.   Since contact with the Europeans, not whole castes but a number of individuals in many castes have given up the old taboo. Vedas are still the most sacred books of the Hindus and yet religious worship, ritual and even Gods have changed since the Vedic times.   Change has been always partial, it has spread very slowly to the strata other than where it started and in most cases it has never encompassed the whole society. This latter fact has made this society appear static to observers. The curious relativistic attitude has never allowed it to make a final choice which involved giving up entirely any of its old ways of behaviour. This has resulted in a museum-like collection and juxtaposition of the old and the new which bewilders outsiders. Each epoch in history has shown some change but the way the society is constituted the effect and significance of these changes have been different from those of similar changes in the societies of the West. The mechanisms of change have been considered briefly in the discussion about communications.

To sum up, (1) the caste is an extended kin-group spread over a definite region. (2) It is never self-sufficient like a tribe because it is specialized generally in one type of occupation. (3) This deficiency is made good by many castes coming together in a village and being bound up in a pattern of mutual duties, obligations and rights. (4) Castes are arranged in a hierarchical order which however leaves some freedom for particular castes to strive for higher positions. (5) The caste society allows new units to come into its web at a time and in a position which is largely indeterminate. (5) Castes remain in peripheral contact with each other, with very large freedom for each caste to follow what it considers to be its traditional pattern. (7) It illustrates the agglomerative character of the whole Hindu society. The society is not a product of continuous splitting of something which was a unit but has arisen out of a loose coming together of many separate cultural entities. (8) Historically this pattern might have existed even before the Aryans came, who merely took it up and perpetuated it. (9) This type of society of juxtaposed groups seems to have arisen at a time when different people came together without any single people being strong enough to impose its political or cultural domination. Most of these societies might have been tribal in nature and each retained its separate character in the new set up. (10) This society continued

H.S.—9

to exist in its old pattern as it had (a) the elasticity to accommodate ever new elements and (b) offered security through a long period of political insecurity and foreign domination. (11) The philosophical systems developed very early in the history of this society, while truly objective, were also at the same time such as to offer a complete justification of the most important aspects of this society. (12) Besides the ideal structure erected by this society its mode of internal articulation made it possible to survive outside attacks and internal schisms.

The greatest challenge to this society has come in the modern times (a) when Britain welded it into one political entity for the first time in its long history, (b) when it gained freedom from the foreign power as one nation and and adopted a democratic constitution, and finally (c) when it is hoping to adopt the modern technology. How it has done it upto now will be considered in the next chapter.

CHAPTER V

THE PRESENT AND THE FUTURE

In a sense the analytical study of Hindu social institutions has been completed. This chapter really poses the problem of what such a society is faced with in modern times and what it has done upto now. Extreme care was needed not to let this chapter become an enumeration of the favourite schemes of the author. The author has tried to take up only a very few of the vast number of questions which can be dealt with. These were chosen only because they illustrate the same point in different ways.

We have seen how the Hindu society has developed in such a way that it has not been able to reject anything. We have called it an agglomerative society. It was also extremely loosely articulated and it has no consciously developed mechanism of resistance. On the philosophical side, this type of social life was based on a conception of reality, a vague indescribable unity called *Brahman* was supposed to be inherent in the manyness of the created universe.

For the first time in its long history, India politically became one. As part of the British Empire, it was loosely connected with countries like Burma and Ceylon. On attaining freedom, it was separated from them. It was also divided from a certain part of its own territory which it had come to regard as a part and parcel of itself. This was Western and Eastern Pakistan. It is not the intention of the author to discuss the political happenings, but only the task which faces what is today a political entity called the Indian Union. When the remaining portion is called a Union, some recognition is given to the fact of many units coming together to form a union. We have thus a

government made up of executive and legislative bodies
at the centre and a number of State governments with their
own executive and legislative bodies.   Upto now most of the
State Governments have belonged to the same party as at
the centre and so a number of common policies are followed
by both; there are however an equal number of cases where
the States and the centre seem to go in different ways.

The main sociological problem in the political, cultural
and economic fields today is that of making room for manyness while not jeopardising the oneness. To take the
political problem first, the Centre never seems to make up
its mind as regards what the units are going to be.   Step
by step the units have become identical with the linguistic
regions and because of the demands for proper demarcation
of the boundaries between the units and the demands for
ever new linguistic units, the Centre seems to feel that the
linguistic units should never have been made.   Together
with this is also involved the problem about a language for
the whole of India and the languages for instruction and
official use in the various States.

It has been pointed out in the previous chapters that
owing to certain historical circumstances like the lack of a
central power or the lack of a central church, the linguistic
regions have been a cultural reality for the people of India.
The effective spread of an in-marrying caste was generally
the extent of the linguistic region.   During the times when
a people spread out of their boundaries, they still came back
for purposes of marriage to their linguistic region.   Also
the modern major languages in India have had written
literature for long periods.   Tamil, the southern-most
language, possesses written literature which is about two
thousand years old, while some languages have a written
literature of only a few centuries.   Sindhi emerged as a
written language not quite three centuries ago.   Some
languages which have a large number of speakers did not
have a written literature.   Some have been uprooted owing
to recent political circumstances from their motherland.
All linguistic areas are zigzagged at the boundaries so that
it is difficult to mark State and regional boundaries through

straight lines or along rivers and mountains. None of the people who speak a particular language and who have had their literary and religious education through it want to give it up. There is hardly any other question which has raised so much controversy as the qestion of a language for India. This question is not simply one about language but is involved with the following problems :— (1) What should be the units of federation of the Indian Republic ? (2) What role should the languages of the States play in administration and in education ? (3) How should the different States communicate with one another and with the world outside? (4) How should recruitment to central services be carried out? () What employment pattern and policy should governments adopt ? (6) What are the cultural and emotional values involved in the language controversy ?

These are but a few of the most important questions involved. The language controversy wages as hotly as ever and is not likely to be solved in an atmosphere of calm consideration. The author outlines a policy below, which possibly has also been swayed by sentiments, but it is given here because it will enable readers to get an idea of the complications which have to be faced in bringing about a transformed society.

When the Indian federation came into being its first shock was the separation of parts of north-east and north-west as a separate Muslim state. India resolved to keep together what remained. It has a constitution by which various States are bound in a federation at the Centre while certain matters are left entirely under the control of the States. Owing to the way in which the British had gone on conquering parts of India and arranging them in "Provinces", it came to happen that most provinces in north India were one-language units and these became, after 1947, the States in the Indian Federation. In the case of the States in south India however, the language regions remained divided and became parts of different states. Such for example was the case as regards Maharashtra, Telangana, Kerala etc. Maharashtra (the region where Marathi language is spoken) was divided among three political units : Western Maharashtra comprising the coastal parts and the western high plateau were in the Bombay Province (of the British time). North-eastern Maharashtra comprising the valley of the Purna river (Berar) and the valleys of Vardha and Vainganga rivers (Nagpur area) were parts of the old Central Provinces and eastern Maharashtra called Marathwada was a part of the old Hyderabad state (Nizam's Dominion). In the same way Andhra (the region of the Telugu-speaking people) was divided between the old Madras Province, Hyderabad state and Mysore state. The linguistic regions in India have a feeling of cultural togetherness which is very strong and which is centuries older than the political States and even than India as a country. These regions have well developed written languages whose literature goes back to several centuries. People who can read and write, though small in number (about 24 per cent according to the 1961 census provisional figures) in different regions represent the leaders in new India and are intensly proud of their language. The linguistic region offered itself as the most popular and natural unit for the new States which were federated. It was so accepted by the Congress leadership before independence but the central government failed to draw up basic principles for demarcating boundaries. Every linguistic region made claims over territories which were disputed by others. Some who had influence at the Centre succeeded for the time being in including in their linguistic areas cities or tracts which could never be so included (inclusion of the famous hill resort of Abu into Gujarat is one such case. It has now been restored to the new Rajasthan State). The Centre went by sentiments rather than on principles and often yielded to pressure groups. The old Bombay Province made up of Gujarat and parts of Maharashtra and Karnatak was allowed to remain for some time. This led to bitterness and agitation, even riots and following these to the ultimate creation of states based largely on the linguistic regions. Even now however

(August 1961) all questions about boundaries have not
been solved.

India with its many developed languages offers analogy
with the continent of Europe rather than with any other
single country, except that, unlike Europe, the linguistic
regions were never political entities. If such multi-
lingual areas are to be governed, some general principles
need to be evolved for marking boundaries, dealing with
linguistic minorities in the nature of enclaves and the
bilingual people near the borders. Deploring the multiplicity of the languages and the pride people take in their own
language and literature and branding it as "linguism" does
not solve the problem. It only exacerbates feelings. The
oneness of language of vast regions can be used as a primary ground for fostering feelings of unity and breaking
caste barriers. The new-found oneness of India can best
be nurtured if all linguistic units feel that they are justly
treated, that their language constitutes no barrier for employment under the Centre and that they can do all they
want to develop their own language. The creation of a
superstate made up of smaller states each speaking a different language[1] raises difficulties about inter-communication,
common recruitment to the services of the central government and maintainance of academic standards for teaching
of scientific and other subjects.

Some years ago the Constituent Assembly passed by
a majority of one vote a resolution making Hindi written
in the Devanagri script the official language of the Union.
This decision has not satisfied many. The present author
being one of them, the whole question is treated here in some
detail.

The qestion is generally dealt with by analogies and/or
through an appeal to sentiments of nationalism or pedago-
gics. Let us examine these one by one. India cannot be
compared with the U.S.A. or U.S.S.R. or Switzerland or

---

[1] There are two Hindi states : Uttar Pradesh and Madhya Pradesh;
Bihar and Rajasthan are also reckoned as Hindi states, as their
languages are very similar to Hindi.

modern Japan in the matter of its political and social situation. The Unites States imposes one language on its multiracial and multi-lingual citizens. This became possible because the English-speaking component was in an overwhelming majority when the States gained independence. The new people who came to the States after that came always as an uprooted people seeking food and refuge and a new life and were ready to give up their language and learn a new one.[2] This uprootedness and fragmentary migration is utterly absent in the case of India. Russia is a land made up of many linguistic regions and many races where regional languages have been given a place in the region and Russian has been adopted as the federal language. Here also the analogy is wrong. Hindi like Russian is spoken by a large number of people but not by the majority of people in India. (About 40% speak Hindi while 60% speak languages other than Hindi according to the 1951 census data). The place of Russian is unique in U.S.S.R. It is the most advanced language, with a unique literature and the modern scientific and technological progress of the whole country is connected with Russian only. Russian-speaking people had taken a major part in the struggle against the Tsarist regime and in founding the new communistic state. In contrast to this, there are many languages in India which have a more developed literature than Hindi, and which claim to be much older than Hindi. It is felt by many that the Hindi-speaking region represents a region backward in modern social and literary awakening.[3] Neither have the Hindi-speaking

---

[2] Even so there are pockets where German or Italian or Norwegian is still spoken.

[3] The provisional figures for the percentage of literates in the different states according to the 1961 census are as follows :—

I	All-India	—	—	23.7
II	Hindi-speaking States			
	Bihar	—	—	18.1
	Madhya Pradesh	—	—	16.9
	Rajasthan	—	—	14.7
	Uttar Pradesh	—	—	17.5

people taken a greater part in the freedom movement than speakers of the other languages.

The analogy with Switzerland fails because of the number of the major languages and the vastness of each linguistic region. Nobody can dream of suggesting that the federal administration be carried on in a dozen different languages!

There is really no analogy at all with Japan. It is mentioned because a number of people point out to Japan and stress the point that Indian languages are capable of taking up all the modern knowledge and technology and transmitting it to people.[4]

There is no doubt at all that the modern Indian languages can take up and transmit all modern knowledge. The issue at stake is not at all about the ability of our languages to do so. The issue is, firstly, one of a common administrative language for a vast multi-lingual area, secondly about keeping abreast of modern knowledge and technology and thirdly about communication between different states and with the outside world. If there were one language current over the whole of India, even with many dialects, that would have been the language of the state; but as it is, the analogy with Japan is entirely inapplicable.

II	Other North Indian States			
	Assam	—	—	25.8
	Kashmir	—	—	10.7
	Orissa	—	—	21.5
	Punjab	—	—	23.7
	West Bengal	—	—	29.1
III	South Indian and Western States			
	Andhra	—	—	20.8
	Gujarat	—..	—	30.3
	Kerala	—	—	46.2
	Madras	—	—	30.2
	Maharashtra	—	—	29.7
	Mysore	—	—	25.3

[4] Speech delivered by Mr. Shrimali, the Central Minister of Education, at Shantiniketan on February 7, 1961 (vide *Times of India* of February 8, 1961).

The making of Hindi into a federal language is felt to be a handicap by non-Hindi people as they think that the examinations for entry into the federal services will have to be in a language other than the mother tongue for a majority of people while for the Hindi-speaking people this will be in the mother tongue.

A solution to this according to the present author and according to some others is to choose, i.e. to continue to use English as the federal language. A historical accident had made it the language of central administration during the colonial period. It has been the language for higher education in all states. It was the language which brought together the leaders from different language-regions for fighting colonial rule and it is the language which contains literature which alone can enable one to understand the present Indian Constitution and the present political trends. Lastly it will serve not only as a medium of communication with the world outside but will be the best medium for access to modern knowledge and technology.

There are people who reject this proposal because they think it unnationalistic to adopt a non-Indian language. This argument cannot be completely answered except in the following ways. The multi-lingual situation in India needs some inter-communicating medium. A language which is not claimed as native tongue by any region in India, is equally near or distant to all and will not arouse mutual jealousies as one of the regional languages will do. It is a very rich language which will make modern knowedge available to us. It will be in due course (and is even now) so transformed and moulded that there will be an Indian variety of English, where possibly articles like *a*, *an* and *the* will be completely dropped and many other changes made.

The adoption of English raises certain other problems too. They and their solution are indicated below :

The present author thinks that if English is adopted as a federal language it should remain only as a second language in the lower stages of education. Every child in India should get all his education including high school and a little after only through one of the regional Indian languages. The author has seen many schools which give all education through the English language and has come in contact with pupils who have been educated in such institutions. Such schools in a large number of cases are run by various Christian missions and do not have efficient teachers for subjects like Mathematics or History or Sanskrit. But the more serious objection is, firstly, that no Indian language is so taught that the pupil is well acquainted with its literature and, secondly, the pupil is brought up in an atmosphere which lacks cultural roots. He does not and cannot take up the culture of any of the western countries like Italy, England, Germany or France because he is in India and remains ignorant of his own cultural roots also. The product which is turned out is such that neither the Westerners, nor the Indians would like to own him. He has an attitude of superiority towards his fellow-Indians and an inferiority complex for being an Indian. Even for those few in India who say that they are born with English as their native tongue it would not be a loss to learn through one indigenous language; it will widen their horizon and sympathy. It is for this reason that the author thinks it necessary for our younger people to learn through the language of the region in which they find themselves.

This raises certain difficulties as regards the children of the central government employees and others who move constantly from region to region. It is necessary for the Government of India in co-operation with the States to establish good schools with residential arrangements in each linguistic region. This need arises not only out of the language difficulty but also out of the fact that the government has a large number of employees from all regions of India who are recruited by means of a public examination. These people at present send their children to the English language schools firstly because a transfer from one region to another will cause no difficulty and secondly because they get a good advantage for employment by learning English. The scheme outlined by the author obviates this possibility and much jealousy and resentment can be eliminated as a consequence.

If the regional language is adopted as the medium of instruction and even if English is made a compulsory second language, many questions will have to be considered. Will all teaching at all stages be through the regional language? At present Indian languages have no good text-books for higher studies to say nothing of reference books. This defect is being slowly remedied, but the text-books turned out by translating *ad hoc* from other languages are of a very low quality. If all studies are through regional languages there would be no independent means to check if standards are kept up. We need for national progress, rapid assimilation and spread of modern science and technology and this object will be helped by instruction through Indian languages at the secondary stage; but at the higher stages it would be best to get the knowledge from original sources. This should not be difficult especially as it is proposed to have English as the second language for all Indian children going up to the secondary stage. The instruction through the regional language with English as the second language can continue till the pupil is about eighteen years old. After that, i.e. at the level of higher education, instruction and examination could be in English with examiners and instructors coming from other regions or even from outside India. Inter-State intercourse at this level should be nurtured in such a way that students can change from one university to another, universities can employ good teachers from any region and for some examinations, examiners also could be appointed from other states or from outside India.

What then will be the place of Hindi in such a scheme? Again the author envisages different levels of communication. A vast number of people will hardly ever go out of their state, but still a large number of non-university people from different linguistic regions will have occasion to meet each other. They very probably will talk and understand a kind of all-India Hindi which no Hindi person would like to think as his language. This Hindi will be transmitted through the agency mostly of the Hindi talking pictures whose songs are already sung all over India. The systematic instruction in Hindi in schools in the non-Hindi regions should not go beyond bare necessity.

What and how should English be taught? Certainly not in the way it is taught now. The drawing up of the syllabus should not be left in the hands of professors of English who are interested in English literature only. English in future in India is going to be an instrument of getting Western knowledge and technology and its teaching will have to be devised in such a way that history of literature or the works of great and ancient writers and poets form but a minimal part of it. The pupil should read voluminously and in varied subjects and a stage will come when he begins to understand what is read or spoken of modern thought.

This kind of language instruction is connected intimately with employment too. The federal government and the state governments are very large employers. All personnel in such departments as Post and Telegraph, Railways, central ministries at Delhi, Ports, research institutions, the three armed services, Income Tax etc. are recruited directly by federal agencies. A great part of the controversy about a common language hinges round the mode and conditions of recruitment of these employees. Delhi the capital of India is located on the borders of three linguistic regions — namely those of Punjabi, Rajastani and Hindi. People outside these linguistic regions feel that these three regions get special advantages as regards employment and enterprise because of the nearness of the capital. These advantages would be enhanced manyfold for the Hindi speaking people if Hindi is made the federal language.

With reference to this aspect of the question, the language commission set up under the chairmanship of the late Shri B. G. KHER in 1956 had asked witnesses if they would be satisfied if after making Hindi the federal language, the central government fixed a quota of central government employees for each linguistic region. This

solution to the problem of competition for central employment was rejected by many but it does open a new approach
to the field.   Each question of social reconstruction involves us in work at different levels.   At the Centre as
also at the State level there are types of employment which
involve almost no specialization at the time of recruitment.
The skills are learned after recruitment.   Such employ-
ments are those of the soldier, the seaman, the ground staff
of the air force, workers in railways and the roads.   Next
to these would come the lowest services in the postal and
telegraph departments and the vast army of peons seen in
various goverment offices.   Some of this recruitment can
be restricted to the area where the services are to be performed while others like the services in the three armed
forces can be deliberately and evenly distributed in the
different States.   The British had created a myth of mar-
tial and non-martial people.   This needs to be exploded.
The recruitment for the fighting services is an indirect
means of bringing home to illiterate or barely literate people from all states the value of some kinds of modern
knowedges like hygiene and medicine.   It also inculcates
discipline.   If military units are so constituted that people
of different castes work together and people of different
regions live and work together, that may break caste
barriers and build up new feelings of one-ness.   For the
prosperity it brings to villages and for the reasons enumerated above this recruitment should be distributed justly
to all States.   Railways and road maintenance of the usual
type can also draw on local services.   Certain services
needing specialization or higher education will need open
competitive examinations where fair play and impartiality
are guaranteed by the complete annonymity of the exa-
minee as far as the examiner is concerned.   However good
interviews and *viva voce* examinations may be, in the present Indian set up the current examination system by
papers seems to fulfill a necessary function.   Just as in the
case of castes and whole groups, even States are not on a
par as regards education.   Recruitment from all States may
not be possible but should be positively encouraged.

For services within a State most recruitment shall be from the State and in such a way that the aspirations of people are given due consideration. A large number of people who were illiterate are getting education. Those who are on a lower level of achievement would feel cheated if their recruitment to services not needing a very high level of schooling is balked by educated people competing for such jobs. Recruitment for a time at least must be such that if a post requires only knowledge of the mother tongue with a smattering of English it should not be filled by a person who is more highly educated. At each stage of educational achievement a large field must be open for employment so that we do not have the rush into the higher stages of education of people who take education simply because they happen to be unemployed.

In this outline of a problem and its likely solution my attempt has been to show how many-sided such problems are and how we have to tackle them so as to give due consideration to our manyness and not to deplore it. But a word as regards the more distant future is also not out of place here. If the above programme comes to fruition, the author envisages an India where each linguistic region will be far richer than it is today in all types of literature; far greater numbers from all castes than today will have access to English; and Hindi of a sort will be generally understood. Then the new generation can think of India in terms we cannot even imagine. The people may then discard English altogether or discard Hindi or discard both and think of new ways of keeping the national unity. The new pattern will depend on our situation and the world situation, but in the meanwhile we shall have given them what we thought was worthwhile, but neither eternal nor immutable.

The greatest challenge posed to the new state is about having a common civil code. The past history and recent history is such that each group had its own traditional rules of behaviour and these rules were applied in the case of each citizen. Muslims, Christians, Jews and Parsees were governed each by his own religious traditions which were uniform for each group. Among Hindus, Jains and Buddhists a single law was not in existence and behavioural rules changed according to time, the part of the country and, in the case of Hindus, according to caste. The Muslim rulers concerned themselves directly with the collection of taxes, but as regards civil disputes, old traditions were followed. Similar was the case as regards the British with a few modifications. An attempt was made to define the law by which Hindus were governed but a uniform code could not emerge as regional differences of patterns were very great.[5] The British on their own initiative made one great change in the prevalent Hindu practice. This was the law against Sutee — the custom of burning widows on the funeral pyre of their husbands. Since then upto the time the British rule ended, some laws were passed in connection with which the initiative was taken by educated Hindus.[6] Dr. AMBEDKAR, the leader of the untouchable Mahar caste, a student of Hindu law and a champion of the down-trodden, was the person who felt it necessary to have a Hindu code applicable to all Hindus.

[5] In Bengal and Bihar the joint family was constituted in the same manner as elsewhere in India but succession, inheritance and the rights in property of a man holding ancestral property were different.

In North India marriage among near kin was not allowed. In almost all of the south, cross-cousin marriage and the marriage of a man to his younger sister's daughter was allowed.

In the north and most of the south the succession was patrilineal, but in Malabar, Travancore and Cochin it was matrilineal. These are but a few examples. For details see *"Kinship Organisation in India"* by the same author, Deccan College Monograph Series, No. 11, Poona, 1953.

[6] The most important among them were:

1. Hindu Widows' Remarriage Act of 1865;
2. The Age of Consent Act;
3. Raising the age of marriage of a Hindu girl to 14;
4. Giving of an equal share with sons in the property of the deceased to the widow.

All these laws except about Suttee and widow remarriage were repealed when parts of the comprehensive Hindu code were passed one after the other beginning with 1955.

He resigned his law-ministership because, among many other reasons, the code as prepared by him could not be passed at once in its entirety in the Indian parliament. Since then however parts of the code are being passed separately. The following important Acts have been passed :[7]

1. The Hindu Marriage Act, 1955.
2. The Hindu Succession Act, 1956.
3. The Hindu Minority and Guardianship Act, 1956.
4. The Hindu Adoptions and Maintenance Act, 1956.

Some of the major changes introduced by these laws in what was formerly regarded as the civil law governing Hindus are :

1. Each Hindu marriage has to be registered, though non-registration is not a proof of non-marriage.
2. Monogamy was enforced by law.
3. Certain degrees of blood relations are not allowed to marry except in south India where kin-marriage is widely practised.
4. Divorce or separation on certain conditions is allowed.
5. The wife and the daughters get equal shares with sons in the estate of a man who dies intestate.

Since the British rule India has had a well codified criminal law which applies to all Indians irrespective of caste or religion.   (Indian Penal Code, Criminal Procedure Code, etc.).   It is worth considering if it cannot become possible to devise a code embodying what the Germans call "*Familien-Recht*" for the whole of India.

The British had no interest in making such a code. After the revolt of 1857 the Queen in a declaration had assured her Indian subjects that her government would not interfere in the religious practices of her new subjects. Neither had the British any particularly urgent motives to generate among the different religions and caste groups a feeling of belonging together or oneness which the new Indian Government is so anxious to create and to nurse.

[7] For details see "*A Text Book of Hindu Law*" by DEOKI NANDAN, Ram Narayan Lal Beni Prasad Publishers, 1960.

As regards changing the old customs the new laws have radically changed the old customs with reference to 1, 2, 4 and 5 in the items of Hindu code quoted above. There cannot be any question about hesitation to interfere with old customs. The interference in the old customs seems to be due to a desire to remove the disabilities from which women suffered i.e. to give equality which the constitution guarantees to all and to allow the dissolution of the marriage bond. The injunction as regards registration seems to be with a view to facilitate collection of statistics while the one about bigamy is due to the influence of Western Christian practices.

There are important agencies besides law which control social behaviour. These are : religion, and the opinion of the group to which a person belongs. Conscience, in a large measure, is internalized mores of the society. This also is an important factor in the control of behaviour. The author thinks that the less legal interference there is, on questions of marriage, the better it is for society, and that the question of the number of people involved in a marital partnership had best be left to be decided by religion, public opinion and private conscience. Similarly, as one third of India allows, or, in many cases prefers cross-cousin marriage, it would not have mattered much if all cousin marriages were allowed by law. Biologically there is no difference between cross- and parallel-cousin marriage. The consequences need not be considered biologically as we are discussing a social event. A few words are however necessary because a number of northern people consider cousin-marriage as a dysgenic practice. The inbreeding is never of a degree carried out in laboratories on animals or by breeders of pet animals and race horses. Large sections of Indian and other populations which have allowed cousin-marriage for many centuries do not show any kind of degeneracy. The historical and cultural record of south India is as brilliant if not more so than that of northern India. Marriage within small castes also leads to inbreeding and that has never been frowned upon by orthodox northerners. It would therefore be quite sufficient if any normal adult person is allowed to marry another provided they are not related as brothers and sisters or parents and children. This taboo is observed by all Indians — Hindu, Muslim, Christians, Jews, Buddhists, Jains and all tribal people. The further restrictions as regards kinship can best be left to the respective religions. This small change would make the law applicable to all communities in India and people won't have to skip from one religion to another[8] to contract a marriage tabooed by a particular group inasmuch as such a marriage would be valid according to the law of the land.

Another item which seems to be redundant in the present code and which makes it inapplicable to all communities in India is the one which makes monogamy compulsory. By the restriction of the law to Hindus only tribals like Todas can practice polyandry and Muslims can practise polygyny. Before this law was passed polygyny was an allowed custom among all Hindus and polyandry was practised by a number of groups from the sub-Himalayan region in the north to Travancore in the south. Except among some rich people and some ruling chiefs and some castes, polygyny was but rarely practised. Polyandry seemed to be on the decline even among the groups among whom it was the pattern for marriage. The law has effectively interfered with the lives of perhaps 1 or 2 per cent people in India but this interference seems unwarranted and unnecessarily creates anger among Hindus and prevents the marriage law from becoming universally applicable.

Everybody knows that the insistence on monogamy in the Hindu Marriage Act of 1955 and in some of the laws passed in a few States prior to that, was due to the refor-

---

[8] The author knows of a respected Hindu Brahmin family in Poona in which children of two brothers have married. As this type of marriage is tabooed among all Hindus, the couple went to Ceylon, became Buddhist and married.

In another case known to the author a Christian woman became Hindu in order to contract a bigamous marriage (the Bigamy Law was not passed then).

mistic zeal of certain sections of Western-educated Hindus, which considered the Christian monogamous pattern of marriage as worth imitating and that monogamy, even legally imposed monogamy, was normally superior to polygyny.

In spite of monogamy having been a tenet of Christianity for nearly 2000 years, cases of bigamy occur all the time and when one reads of such cases i.e. those that come before the courts, one has the feeling that the practice has a certain constant percentage among Western people.

Many more people in the West are having more than one partner during the course of their married lives than those who practised polygyny in India. Only, they take on a new partner after divorcing the old one so that they do not have more than one partner at the same time. However, from a moral point of view the author does not find any difference between two partners at different times and two partners at the same time. The number and intensity of social problems arising in both cases seem to be of the same order. Behaviour of the highest moral standard also is possible in both types of situations. Changing a partner after divorce is a social phenomenon much discussed in Western literature and sociology and I need not discuss it here. I would however like to refer to some cases in India involving polygyny which were personally known to me, which will illustrate the moral choice involved (see Appendix).

Among some castes the number of people having more than one wife is greater than among others. Such is the case for example among the cotton and wool weaver caste. The work unit is the family and to each wife is allotted a certain work before the yarn is ready to be set on the loom. Sometimes agriculturists had wives living on farms situated at a distance from each other and travelled between and lived regularly at the two households.

A very large majority of women in India have wifehood as an honorable way of earning a living. Even in polygynous India marrying a man who already had a wife was considered but a second choice. This was done (1) if a girl was poor or (2) if a man was very rich or (3) if a girl could not easily get married as she did not have good looks or in rare cases (4) if the girl's parents or family got money or other assistance from the groom's family. Many a girl has willingly married a rich man with a wife rather than a poor bachelor who had nothing to offer. After all, there will always be people ready to compromise on one item or the other in their life's situation and polygyny is one such compromise allowed by certain societies.

The law is especially irksome because it does not apply to some people e.g. to Muslims. If a thing is forbidden because on the basis of some moral principles it is felt to be bad, it must be forbidden to all people and not just a few. Muslims are in no way gainers by being exempted from this law, but this gives ground for Hindu propagandists to have a grievance. In a society divided deeply by castes and religions, even such a small ground for alleged preferential treatment need not exist and from this view point too the monogamy section in the Hindu Marriage Act seems to be uncalled for.

The thing which was really wrong as regards polygyny was that it was imposed without choice on many women. What was needed to remove social injustice would be a law providing a way of escape and monetary compensation for a partner not willing to live in such a household. It would suffice to make that a ground for divorce and compensation.

The same arguments apply to polyandrous practices too. Taking all these things into consideration it should have been possible to devise a law governing marriage and dissolution of marriage which would be applicable to all Indian citizens.

The same applies to the law about inheritance and succession. Parliament has already modified the ancient Hindu practice inasmuch as following the Constitution it has given an equality with men to the women of a family. As regards this law the prescriptions differ according to (a) whether one is a member of a joint or a non-joint family, (b) whether one is a member of a patrilineal or a matrilineal family and (c) whether one is governed by some modifications of the above two types of families. If the law is made general and universal it will not need many modifications, exceptions and other similar complications. It should enunciate certain principles for the patrilineal type of joint family and others for the matrilineal type. The Muslims follow the patrilineal pattern except in Travancore, where like their Hindu brethren they have large matrilineal families. If by providing for them and for the Jews and Parsees one or two more types are added for determining succession and inheritance, it would certainly not make the law more complicated than it is today. This attempt is worth making. A common civil code for all the citizens of India would be a challenge to the spirit of tolerance and liberalism taught by the ancient Hindus and loudly voiced as a precious cultural possession by the present Hindus. It will be a symbol of a new unity for the people of India.

Another change from the old Hindu practice in the new law of succession is complete deprivation of any rights for maintenance of a concubine and her children. According to old practice and legal decisions a concubine and her children had certain rights in the estate. The author has known cases in which this right was enforced by a court of law during the British times, because the Hindu law as administered at that time was based on the injuctions of the Smṛtis. In the new law, all mention of a concubine and her children has been dropped from the list of heirs and successors. In the author's opinion this deprivation compares with the action of Abraham in setting his concubine Hagar and her child Ishmail in the desert. A concubine is a woman who lives with a man for the whole of his life and one would expect that he should be made to provide for her and her children. This omission goes against natural justice, serves no moral principle and unnecessarily restricts the law only to one community.

Having considered two major questions vitally affecting the unity of India, I propose to deal with some more problems of the same kind in the remaining part of this chapter.

Among India's people there are some who do not kill or eat the meat of any kind of animal, while at the other extreme, are people who will kill and eat almost any living thing. Between these two types of groups, are those who will eat and/or kill only particular types of animals and some who have a definite taboo towards some animals due to alleged evilness or sacredness. The problem is fraught with deep feelings nurtured through generations. It is also connected with the needs of a modern state and an evergrowing population which uses land indiscriminately. Indian agricultural economy is dependent on seasonal rainfall and conservation of soil. Both these are adversely affected by destruction of forests and trees and overgrazing by animals. No animal is as destructive to trees as the goat. This animal has acquired a sentimental value in recent times because it was called the "poor man's cow" by Mahatma Gandhi. The poor man however keeps a goat because it eats the foliage of all the surrounding trees. The national loss it entails is far greater than the little milk or meat it gives. It needs to be restricted and perhaps altogether banned from certain areas as the state of Israel has recently done. The cattle pose another problem. It is using land for fodder which is needed for grain; through overgrazing it lays soil bare which is then washed away in the monsoon rains. In certain parts of Maharashtra (Sangli, Satara) cattle which was let loose because it was too old to work has reverted back to a wild state. Such cattle move in great herds and have been eating with impunity the harvest of the farmers. Cattle which is let loose right in the midst of cities in the name of a god or a temple are a menace to school-going children. The bullock might be replaced in work through mechanical contrivances like the tractor and the bus. The number of bullock carts plying on roads has gone down since the introduction of trucks and buses. The female of the buffalo is ousting the cow as milch-cattle. Whatever the situation, one can make laws for preventing slaughter of animals in an indiscriminate way and publicly, but in a multi-cultural state only one animal, say the cow or bullock, cannot be singled out to form the basis of state policy. Active protection of the feelings of a community must be coupled with due freedom of others.

The way of life of the Indian society described in the first four chapters has been such that groups have lived side by side without merging. This, coupled with a philosophy which teaches that God can meet different people in different ways according to their hearts' desires, has resulted in a way of thought and behaviour which the Hindus like to call "tolerance". If there were real tolerance based on understanding of and sympathy for the values of other groups, the experiment of living together would have come up against no difficulties at all. But today the social, and therefore the economic and political life of the people is vitiated by distrust, hatred, jealousy and rivalries for groups other than one's own. From the smallest group to the largest the battle is fought with arson, rape, killing and robbery and generally under the guise of moral indignation or some moral principle. Modern democracy and elections have given a new edge to old antagonisms. History, mythology, statistics are misused in these campaigns and young people reading distorted accounts of the activities of people belonging to certain other groups get heated to the point of organizing or joining "self-defence" or "service" groups with military discipline. No party hesitates to make use of group loyalties and group rivalries and at the same time all parties are loudly denouncing "casteism and communalism".[9]

The groups which are locked in this struggle are religious groups like the Hindus, Muslims, Parsees, Christians, Sikhs etc. Among Hindus, the untouchables against the touchables; religious sects like Lingayats and

---

[9] The author has witnessed two periods of such group hatreds. One was in Germany, just when Hitler was coming to power, the second was just before and after the murder of Mahatma Gandhi in India.

non-Lingayats (in Karnatak); caste-clusters like Brahmins and non-Brahmins (all over India, but especially in the whole of the country south of the river Narmada); within non-Brahmins one type of caste-cluster against others (for example Maratha versus Mali, and Maratha versus Leva in Maharashtra); within the untouchable group one untouchable caste against another (e.g. Mahars versus Chambhars in Maharashtra); and lastly the tribal people versus the non-tribal.

As regards rivalries between groups one of the arguments put forward is to represent the rival group as aliens. The Hindus like to represent the Muslims as both foreigners and, because of partition, as traitors. The non-Brahmins like to think of the Brahmins in the same way. The scheduled castes have taken up new names like Adi-Dravida (the original Dravidians) or Adi-Karnataka (the original inhabitants of Karnatak) to suggest that all the others were new-comers. With regard to the demand of the Muslims to have a separate state, one may regret the event, but one cannot call it a traitorous act. It has already been stated that India was never politically one until the British brought it under one rule. Though the Mughal power had almost waned before the British took over, still the emperor at Delhi was officially acknowledged as suzerain even by the Marathas. The Muslims had lived in India as conquerors for nearly a thousand years. Bengal and Sind were taken by the British rulers from Muslim rulers. Sind had historically become a Muslim kingdom as early as the 10th century. During the British rule there were many Hindu-Muslim riots, though for a time both the groups had combined in a common struggle against the British. During the last stages of this struggle however the Muslims came to realise that they who were once rulers would always be fated to remain a minority in the Indian Central Government and chose to break away. This separation can be deplored; the events following it were awful on both sides, but still the parting cannot be represented as a traitorous act. Neither does it now justify the demand that those who have stayed behind (and who have no other home except India), be deemed foreigners and hated. A ceaseless campaign goes on in a section of the Indian Press which represents every criminal act of a Muslim as a crime of the whole community and young people are incited against Muslims.[10]   A similar campaign goes on, on the other side of the border with equal zest against the Hindus. The same technique is employed in other cases too. Mahatma Gandhi was murdered by a man belonging to the Chitpavan Brahmin caste in Maharashtra. This occasion was seized upon by the Maratha community to burn down and plunder Brahmin houses, an orgy in which thousands of families were rendered houseless and women on some occasions were also assaulted. The Government has not been able to reduce communal tensions because (i) it uses communal loyalties and hatreds to fight its political campaigns just as others do, (ii) it did not institute or allow impartial inquiries into arson, looting and rape occurring in communal rots of all types and (iii) on no occasion does it publish authoritative facts and figures about the loss of life, property and honour arranged according to communities. This last omission is made use of by partisans to represent that the looting and arson was either of a negligible nature and occasioned by the moral indignation felt by their side (as in the case of the Maratha atrocities against Brahmins), or were committed by the other community (as in the case of the Jabalpur riots). The public must know the facts so that the saner elements can comment on them and people can be made to think. Innumerable funds exist in India for the benefit of castes and religious groups and it is necessary that these should all be merged into a general fund for the benefit of all those who are needy and deserving. Contributions to funds intended to benefit castes or communal groups should be stopped by law.

The legislation passed or intended to be passed by certain State governments, though given high-sounding names

[10] The recent (March 1961) press campaign against the Muslims after the Jabalpur riots is a case in point.

(e.g. socialistic pattern of society, co-operative farming, prohibition etc.) seems to hit certain castes or religious groups far more adversely than others. The Bombay law of prohibition affected the Parsee community very much and many felt that it was a blow aimed at a rival group. In the same way the legislation about a ceiling on land holdings as proposed at first in Maharashtra (February 1961) appeared to many to be intended against the western Maharashtra Mali caste. The rivalry between two groups of capitalists does not merely remain a personal rivalry but becomes simultaneously a caste and religious rivalry, for example between Marwaris and Parsees. When children belonging to different communities quarrel, the event threatens to develop into a major communal riot.

This is not a thing which will yield to oratory. Patient re-education is needed, not only for the masses, but also for the political parties and their leaders contending for power in the political arena. A moral code for political conduct needs to be evolved and strictly adhered to by all parties. People must recognise that quarrels between groups run on the same lines, that the Hindu-Muslim quarrel is not intrinsically different from the Brahmin-non-Brahmin or the Maratha-Mali quarrels. The one cannot be represented as something deeper and more fundamental than the others. Neither can one group claim to have more right to be called Indian than another group. The Muslims have contributed to what we call our culture and civilization. So have the Brahmins, the agricultural castes, the untouchables and the tribals. The long and varied history of the land must be learnt in an unbiassed way.

In Indian epistemology, moral philosophy and literature the concept of memory called 'Smṛti'[11] plays a role which needs to be remembered in this context. 'Smṛti' is the principle of recognition, the principle of continuity in a person's life and the principle of continuity between one birth and the next. Thus each act of cognition is recogni-

---

[11] This *Smṛti* is different from the *Smṛti* literature referred to in other chapters. *Smṛti* here means simply "memory".

tion, each birth is a re-birth and each friendship and attraction, a resumption of an old relationship.

A man should remain conscious till the moment of death, remembering what he has done and what he wishes to become. Memory is dormant, sensed rather than actively felt; when a man remembers his previous existence he is *jāti-smara*. When he remembers all the past as leading to the present, and has no desires to take him into another birth, then final release is achieved. This doctrine applies to a society and its culture also. Communication over a time-span through memory—oral or written—binds a society together. For final release the memory must be clear and untainted by revulsion or love. Today must be viewed as made up of all past. India to a very large extent has a continuity with its past, but portions of its populations cherish some aspects of the past and reject others. A complete unclouded memory alone will lead to sanity, partial amnesia will not do. Some link their past to 'Aryan' Vedic people only, forgetting that Hinduism today is largely non-Vedic. Some look with hatred on the Muslim period, forgetting that our daily life contains much that we have taken from the Muslims. Some will wipe out all memory of the British. The Dravidians deny and denounce everything 'Aryan' or 'Sanskritic'. The northerners forget that nobody knows what racial mixture the Vedic people represented and that we all are mongrels. The pre-Dravidians, the Aryans, the Dravidians, the unknown speakers of Mundari languages, all have contributed to our physical and cultural make up and it will not do to forget any of this ancestry or reject parts of it. Every one of us is all that. It will not do to hate our past or be ashamed of it.

The Indian society is trying to work out modes of living together by breaking old caste loyalties. But it seems today (the year 1961) that the government and the people are both strengthening the old bonds and creating new islands of separateness. A few examples will illustrate this. The Constitution, in order to give protection and encouragement to those who have remained economically backward and socially isolated, has drawn up schedules of the tribal people and people of certain castes as those deserving and needing specially favoured treatment. That is why these castes and tribes are called "scheduled castes" and "scheduled tribes". If a person belongs to one of these, he is ensured a certain representation in the state and federal legislatures and a certain favoured treatment in the matter of employment under the state by means of reservation of ports. Also, children of parents belonging to these two groups are given financial help from state funds for their education and sometimes a little land is also granted to such people. The majority of persons belonging to the scheduled castes and tribes are in dire need of these extra amenities but the way these are given perpetuates social segregation. Sometimes these advantages are claimed and enjoyed by people who do not need them. This abuse of the constitutional provisions has now led to a modification of the procedure to get financial help. It is now necessary to produce a certificate from certain government officials about the financial condition of the family before such help is given.

The listing in the schedules in the Constitution is sought to be continued by the people who are classified as backward.[12]

Primitive groups which did not know of one another's existence and which could not communicate with one another because of linguistic differences, have been shown a new basis of group formation through the fact that they all belong to the "scheduled tribes". There is an administrative machinery to see that specially favoured treatment is given to them. This machinery employs big and small administrators, mainly from the non-scheduled groups, whose interest it is to keep the separate administration of the scheduled castes and tribes going. In the very nature

---

[12] Recently the government of Mysore represented to the Central Government that 90% of the population of that state was backward and so the state should receive extra help from Central funds. A similar claim was made in Parliament by the representatives from Orissa.

of things the extra help given to backward people is supposed to last for a while until the backwardness dis-
appears.   Institutions set up to carry out this work must
also have a short span of life.   But as students of sociology
know, institutions once set up have a tenacious life and the
very people employed to destroy backwardness may help to
prolong it.

If one takes into account all these things, one can see
that national unity or togetherness may be jeopardised by
keeping up these schedules.   On the other hand it is necessary that the kind of specially favoured treatment referred
to above should continue for backward people.   It is therefore necessary to legislate not in terms of certain castes
and tribes but in more general terms, e.g. economic or educational backwardness, which would become applicable to
all citizens.   The beneficiaries can be designated as coming
from certain economic groups and/or from certain under-
developed rural areas.   No needy and backward person
should be prevented from getting help, but then he need
not necessarily and exclusively belong to certain "named"
groups.   The whole legislation must be such that it is
applicable to all citizens of India irrespective of creed or
colour and it must not be profitable for people to belong
nominally to particular and distinct groups like castes,
tribes or religious communities.

Many state governments have generously supported
projects of building decent shelters for people of scheduled
castes.   The author has visited some of these new colonies
which bear names like Gandhi-Nagar or Nehru-Nagar.
These are situated at some distance from the rest of the
town and have given rise to a new consciousness of separateness and the power of voting in a block.

Sometimes government effort to give aid to the poor
results in excluding those who need it most.   The author
has pointed out how this happens.[13]   The village welfare

---

[13] *Evaluation report, on the working of the Welfare Extension Pro-
    jects of the Central Social Welfare Board,* Planning Commission,
    1959.

centres started by the Central Welfare Board are housed many times in rented buildings or buildings donated by some rich man of a village. People who can rent part of their house, or who can donate a whole house belong always to the higher castes and the houses are situated right in the midst of the village. In many cases such houses cannot be entered by the untouchables or are so far from the untouchable quarters that they cannot give effective help in education and medicine to those who most need it. This also adds up to distrust and resentment felt by one group towards another.

Literacy, ease of travel and newspapers are helping in creating new types of castes. Pseudo-anthropology has led to attempts at amalgamation of castes which bear similar names and have similar occupations. The potters have a central body to amalgamate all potter castes of Maharashtra. Sometimes such associations exist for the whole of India. There is an all-India shepherd union. These are not primarily trade unions but attempts to extend the kinship circle represented by a caste. At the meetings of such associations resolutions are passed such as " 'sub-castes' should be abolished and by inter-marriage the unity of the caste should be restored — a unity which was disturbed by the splitting of the original one caste into many sub-castes."

Such attempts at 'uniting' sub-castes sometimes result in new quarrels. For example, the "Brahman Sabha" in Bombay used to recognise the "Brahmin-hood" of certain castes only and has given deep offence to many castes known as some kind of Brahmins.

Most often the intended unity is a unity in name only. It is useful for fighting elections but when the question of marriage comes up, over ninety per cent of marriages are within the own caste[14] in urban areas and almost cent per cent in rural areas.

---

[14] *Vide* (a) Report on inter-group relations by KARVE and DAMLE shortly to be published by the Deccan College, Poona and (b) figures in the survey of Poona marriages of 1959 being compiled by a student of this institution, Shri MOKASHI. Both these are referred to before.

The population of each caste and its distribution, its hereditary occupation and present economic and educational status all need to be taken into account when plans are made for the advancement of one caste or of a whole nation as the following examples will make clear — The untouchables constitute about 10% of the population of Maharashtra. Among the untouchable castes the Mahar caste-cluster makes up over 70%. This Mahar population is scattered over most of the villages of Maharashtra. In any village there may be from one to about twenty houses of this community, as usual set apart from the whole of the village. Among untouchables, castes like Chambhar and Holar (leather workers), Mang (tanners and rope-makers) have occupations which require some skill and are useful even today to the villagers. The Mahars on the other hand represent a caste of village servants, who are not specialists of any type.[15] Their occupation used to be that of messengers, watchmen, removers of dead cattle and attendants on revenue officers. All these are very dispensable services. Their refusal to carry away dead cattle because of the stigma attached to it has antagonised them from the villagers. They do not take part in the religious ceremonies because of their recent mass conversion to Buddhism. Even before this, they had migrated in very large numbers to the cities as industrial labourers. In the villages quite a number still remain, as there was not enough employment for them in the cities and also because they, as a whole community had a bit of land given to them in the village plus a certain small share of food-grains produced by the village. This latter the villagers are now refusing to give. The land-holding also has been abolished by a recent Act passed in the Bombay legislature with the full consent and agreement of this community. This has snapped their last link with the villages. Under these circumstances their position is very pitiable. Some are still in the ancestral villages but are so harassed by the unsympathetic treatment at the hands

---

[15] Except as village musicians.

of the rest of the villagers that they are finding it almost impossible to continue there.

In my opinion the best solution to this problem is to help the Mahars in the villages to be transferred to urban industrial centres where they can not only become absorbed in the economic development, but where it is easier to break down the segregation to which they are subjected in villages. There is a possibility of at least the richer of them living in localities where touchables live.

It may not be possible to absorb all such people in the cities or towns. It would then be necessary to put them on government dole on condition that they must accept any job that becomes available. The Governments in all the States are spending enormous amounts over many projects and it is possible to give jobs to such people there.

This is a solution which seems to run counter to that offered by other agencies. Vinobaji Bhave for example has a programme of taking away land from bigger land-holders and distributing it to the landless. In this context expressions like 'the landless' and 'land-hunger' are often used. This programme not only envisages giving land to the landless but also hopes to restore back to the villages their ancient vigour and self-sufficiency. The author has had the opportunity of seeing the working of this programme on some occasions and ventures to say that it has not only not achieved the solution of existing problems but added new complications. There is not enough land or enough bigger landholders in Maharashtra to give sufficient land to all the landless. Distributing about five acres of land to a family only adds to the number of semi-starving people. It gives a little land to people who have absolutely no capital to put in their holdings and who in most cases either have no experience in farming or have lost ancestral lands through carelessness or extravagence. The author has seen such land leased to other farmers by their new owners. If a few Mahars get land in this way they will find it difficult to live in the village as the other villagers are not well disposed to them.

H.S.—11

The author has observed villages and made surveys of some for the last twenty-five years and finds two things— (1) the village represents such a narrow circle of social intercourse that life is vitiated by hereditary feuds and rivalries and it represents a stagnant society in which new ideas do not enter easily.   It is the stronghold of superstition and witchcraft.   (2) Except for a few bigger villages the communities are too small to accommodate artisans or people rendering necessary occasional services.   Owing to insufficiently of clientele and unnecessary involvements in the feuds of the majority community, minority groups are happier living in market towns.   Such market-towns serve between twenty to thirty villages, have a goodly number of carpenters, smiths, barbers, rope-makers, eating houses and sometimes a cinema.   Potters display their wares on market days, and merchants have shops to sell cloth and other articles of consumption.

Such market-towns are so attractive to villagers that almost every able-bodied villager goes to the market-town fifty-two weeks of the year.   Even when he has nothing to buy or to sell he makes it a point to go walking anywhere upto six miles and back to be at the market.[16]   He goes there to meet people, to exchange gossip, to get away from the monotony of his village for at least one day in the week.

The trend seems to be for many castes to leave the villages and settle in the market town.   It has been pointed out that life in India was lived between two cells — (1) the caste and (2) the village.   Every one feels it necessary to break one cell.   The author thinks that the other cell needs to be broken too — is in fact on the way to a break.   It is futile to try to restore it.   It would be better to accept and strengthen the new model of villages grouped round a prosperous market-town with one or more small industries to offer employment, medical care in the shape of hospital and a dispensary, education in the shape

[16] In Mountainous tracts like Mahableshwar in the Satara district of Maharashtra, villagers climb over 2000 feet and walk five miles to go to the market place on the market day.

of good schools and entertainment. Such towns need to be connected to villages by good all-weather roads on which buses can ply. The villages will be made up of agriculturists keeping cattle and poultry and the town will be made up of many castes representing artisans, labourers and professionals of all types. Roads would make intercourse easy and continuous and life will be confined not just to one village but to a neighbourhood made up of a town and several villages.

The social aim must not be isolation but building up of larger communities where people can mingle in free uncompulsive intercourse.

Vinobaji BHAVE's way is the easier way. It does not cost government either thought or money to take away from some and give to others. The other way would cost money and need a lot of organization and building up. The former way also fits in with ideas of what is considered as social justice under the name of socialism. It gives the satisfaction of doing something for the poor without really doing anything at all. Landlessness is a condition which is common to many people in a state and need not be considered an evil.[17] Land-hunger is another expression which merely means unemployment. The landless masses never possessed land, there is not enough land to go round. What is needed is employment for these people away from the old stagnant villages. Instead of acknowledging the problem in its entirety, distribution of inadequate strips of land to families merely perpetuates the old situation of utter poverty and general backwardness.

In the zeal to restore the old system and introduce people to democracy, committees of villagers are sought to be created on the basis of elections. These committees have the old name of 'Panchayat' (the village council). The elections have created new means of coercion, bribery

---

[17] The traditional form of which is best described by Shri ATRE in his "*Gaon-gada*" reissued by the Gokhale Institute of Politics and Economics, Poona (in Marathi).

and rivalry. The Panchayats which work well for the good of the village are exceptions rather than the rule. In this context the whole question of democracy and vote needs a short discussion.

The Indian Union is called a democracy. Democracy assumes that a normal adult individual is capable of exercising choice as to who shall rule. A further implication of this belief is that every normal adult is capable of holding certain positions of power and direction. If both the propositions are worked together, then it should not bring harm to society if the principle of choice is used together with other principles like rotation by age or the principle of chance. An example may be given to make this clear. In the villages the government is now trying out a new experiment of local rule through the local authority of the Panchayat. Elections often lead to bitter feelings and factions which get perpetuated in the numerically small and physically restricted environment of a village. Minority communities are either drawn into such factions or play a disproportionately important role as their few votes can tip the balance of power. Under such circumstances would it not be better to reserve Panchayat membership to a certain age group of the whole population and by rotation? Village affairs are something which every adult can be supposed to understand and such a procedure may reduce (1) tensions and (2) intrusion of larger political quarrels into the village. In its turn it might lead to the tacit understanding that certain issues can be left out of the sphere of power-politics. The head of the Panchayat can be chosen by drawing lots.[18]

Power and status are different but go hand in hand on many occasions. Actual power is enjoyed by a person but those who are relatives, or friends or party members get a status and through it a certain amount of power. If power itself were distributed widely and care were taken

[18] It was reported in the "Sakal" newspaper of April 7, 1961 that appointments of some temporary lower staff in the Mahableshwar Municipality (Maharashtra State) were made by drawing lots from among the applicants.

that it did not remain in the same hands long, those not in power can be asked to await their turn.

Transfer of power whether from one group to another or from one individual to another and retirement from active work pose very difficult organizational problems. Succession to the Mughal throne was through blood, but this need not necessarily be so. Power structures of all types are found dependent on sex and age. Among Hindus almost every man marries and finds himself in the power position of a husband and father. A woman becomes a mother or mother-in-law. There are rules for succession so as to avoid domestic crises. There are rules of retirement for all types of specialized services like doctors, teachers, drivers of public vehicles etc. What is lacking is a rule for retirement from non-specialized services like the Sarpanch (foreman of village council) or the ministers who can be "elected" again and again. Vote and election cannot be termed devices which reflect popular will or enable the poor or weak to fight on terms of equality with either the rich or the powerful. If human justice is the aim, and equality the credo, then the machine of political power must be worked in such a way that we use all devices known to us for distribution of power.

Democracy is after all a means to secure social justice and freedom. Election is one of the means of securing democracy. But the vote becomes a saleable commodity and the election a device to retain power by buying votes. Social justice and human freedom are such complicated things that one standard type of means is crude and inadequate to secure them. We must not forget the goals in the zeal for the means. If the goals are thought over deeply some of the democratic and reformistic zeal will wane. "Each man serves his own God who is shaped by his heart's desire" is one of our ancient tenets. We shall allow people this ultimate freedom as long as the freedom of one does not become the bondage of another. This thought will hold our hands from making laws telling people what to eat or drink and how to live or to regulate their lives in detail.

In India from the north to the south are nomadic
castes which wander most of the year. The author has
seen them on the frozen banks of the upper reaches of the
Himalayan rivers, on the plains of northern Gujarat, in
the deep south and lastly in Maharashtra. Some of them
herd cattle (buffaloes), some are sheep and camel herders,
some tend flocks of geese, some herd pigs, some are hun-
ters. They beg a little, steal a little and work a little.
They are on the move most of the time with the whole
family and all belongings and sleep under the stars. The
whole world is theirs. The foolish agriculturist with backbreaking work creates wealth which lies unfenced and un-
protected for them to steal from. They have resisted all
attempts to settle them. The new government with its reformistic zeal is after them and these last free people of
the world may succumb. May an anthropologist plead that
as worshippers of many gods we try to find ways for these
nomads to live as they choose, not to build houses or settle
down? Let us not tie down life to one model leading into
one inevitable blind alley of drab comfortable domesticity.

Poor people seem to have played a peculiar role in
society at all times. They have provided the means for
others for displaying piety and bounty. They have provided the means to exercise power by being made slaves
and in recent years have become a pawn in the game of
power where they are used as a pretence to seize power.
The poor people themselves have rarely the opportunity to
plan their own lives to their liking.

The variety of behavioural patterns represents a multiplicity of groups and their ways of life. There are some
aspects of this life. (a) the groups, though belonging to
one society, have become in certain respects mutually exclusive and antagonistic; (b) the life of all groups, viewed
together, offers an immense range of alternatives, making
each aware that ethical values can be realised in different
ways and that a large number of things are mere matters
of tradition without any ethical content *per se;* (c) the
same sense has kept this society polytheistic, and at the
same time certain cruel practices, which were never univer-

sal, used for worship or propitiation of deities have been
given up.

In the attempt to build a new sense of unity, group-
life is viewed with suspicion, but smaller groups are necessary for people for the immediate warmth of fellowship.
Large groups on the national level tend to demand that individuals are linked to no other groups. In such cases
even primary companionships become impossible through
mutual suspicion or tend to lose their support from society
and the individual is doomed to a loneliness in which the
only means of recognition and self-fulfilment become either
power or wealth. Neither must the new attempt at unity
suppress all patterns but one. Would it not be better to
ask ourselves the difficult question of how to foster a feeling of unity without unnecessarily suppressing the multiplicity? The task is difficult as it involves a conscious
appreciation by all political leaders and social reformers
that the new principles that they may want to introduce
are not absolute unshakeable tenets of a monotheistic creed,
but variable means of bringing about greater justice and
efficiency into a social order.

APPENDIX TO CHAPTER V

Folk-tales and songs have described the relations between co-wives, as also those between step-mothers and step-children. The literature on the subject dates back to the Atharva Veda, which records certain magic formulæ for making a rival barren.[19] The advice given by a father to his daughter in a famous verse by Kalidas[20] was to behave in a friendly fashion towards co-wives. The Indian literature, because of the prevalence of polygyny shows a treatment of the eternal triangle, two women and a man, entirely different from that found in Western literature.[21] A Marathi saint-poet[22] has vividly described the sorry plight of a man who was foolish enough to have two wives. Since ancient times rulers and men of powerful families have been known to contract polygynous marriages for the sake of political alliances. Polygyny was a method of displaying wealth. There were, however, more personal factors involved in such marriages. The following cases, known personally to the author are described in detail as they illustrate some of those personal factors which led people to practise polygyny.

Barrenness or the absence of a male child led oftenest to the man marrying a second wife. In many instances the first wife herself took the initiative in arranging the second marriage of her husband. This type of marriage was not confined to any particular economic class.

A. The wife of a man in the author's kinship group gave birth to a daughter and had to have an operation performed, which made it impossible for her to have any more

---

[19] *Atharva Veda*, 7, 35(36).

[20] KALIDASA'S *Shākuntala*, Act 4.

[21] e.g. *Svapnavasavadattā*, by BHASA.

[22] TUKARAM, *Abhang* (Marathi), Bombay, Govt. Central Press, 1950, I, p. 428, (No. 1237).

children. She then took the lead in finding a new bride for her husband and lovingly brought up the children of her co-wife. This incident took place 70 years ago.

B. This is a more recent example, about 25 years back. The wife of a rich business man, who also had considerable landed property, did not get a child for several years after their marriage. The husband took his wife to many famous gynaecologists in different parts of the world and they all declared that she was incapable of having children. She then persuaded her husband to marry a second wife, herself chose a suitable bride and had the good fortune of seeing the co-wife give birth to an heir to the property. She always used to say, "An adopted son is a complete stranger and has no connection with me. The son of a co-wife is the son of my husband and is thus closer to me."

C. Both parents of a woman, who had been married for some years, died one after the other and she took over the guardianship of her younger sister. This young girl was attending a college and came to live with her married sister and her husband during the vacations. The elder sister was busy with her household duties and the care of her young children and the younger sister found herself very often in the company of her brother-in-law. Some time later, the elder sister discovered to her dismay that her younger sister was pregnant by her husband. After giving the matter her serious consideration, she thought it best to get her husband to marry her younger sister. As luck would have it, the man died some years later and the younger sister took service in a school and the two sisters brought up their children in a joint household. If the elder sister had driven away her younger sister in a fit of rage, the life of the latter would have been utterly ruined and probably her own domestic life might also not have been any better than it was after her sister became her co-wife.

D. A man of a respected and educated family married a woman from another equally respected and progressive family. It so happened that the woman had some physical handicap which made it impossible for the couple to lead a normal married life. Under the circumstances the man married a second wife. Although he could have got his first marriage declared null and void and perhaps sent away his first wife to her parental home, he did nothing of the kind. On the contrary, the first wife remained in his house, retained her place of honour as the senior lady of the house and even exercised some authority on the co-wife in the matter of her accompanying the husband on social occasions. The second wife died after a few years and the man, who had now become fairly senior in his profession, married a highly educated lady who took part in various social movements in her town. Both of them were well thought of in their region and earned the respect and goodwill of their fellow-citizens. In fact the way the man had treated the first wife was always considered as an honourable and considerate way. The first marriage took place about 50 years ago.

E. A few years ago, before the law against bigamy was passed the author met a young girl who boarded the train at the railway station of Ahmednagar. An elderly couple had come to see her off. Usual inquiries elicited the fact that the couple were the young girl's parents-in-law. The girl had come from Kalyan, near Bombay, where her husband was working, to help nurse the father-in-law who had been very ill. After about a month's stay she was going back to her husband. The author asked the obvious question about who cooked for the husband during her absence and the young girl answered, that this was taken care of by her co-wife who also happened to be her elder sister. The young girl further informed the author during the conversation that the elder sister and she were deeply attached to each other. The elder sister after her marriage found out that her husband and the parents-in-law were very good and kind people and at the same time quite well off. She had therefore prevailed upon her parents to give the younger sister as bride to the same man and begged her husband to consent to this arrangement. The younger girl told me that the sisters were very happy together, staying by turns or together with the husband and visiting the parents-in-law's house either in turns or all three together.